STACY AGUILERA

SPORTS HEROES AND LEGENDS

Muhammad Ali

Read all of the books in this exciting,
action-packed biography series!

Hank Aaron	*Michael Jordan*
Muhammad Ali	*Sandy Koufax*
Lance Armstrong	*Michelle Kwan*
Barry Bonds	*Mickey Mantle*
Roberto Clemente	*Shaquille O'Neal*
Joe DiMaggio	*Jesse Owens*
Tim Duncan	*Jackie Robinson*
Dale Earnhardt Jr.	*Alex Rodriguez*
Lou Gehrig	*Wilma Rudolph*
Mia Hamm	*Babe Ruth*
Tony Hawk	*Ichiro Suzuki*
Derek Jeter	*Tiger Woods*

SPORTS HEROES AND LEGENDS

Muhammad Ali

by Carrie Golus

BARNES & NOBLE

NEW YORK

For Patrick, Ben, and Alex

Cover photograph:
© Bettmann/CORBIS

Sports Heroes and Legends™ is a trademark of Barnes & Noble Publishing, Inc.

2006 Barnes & Noble Publishing

ISBN-13: 978-0-7607-7518-9
ISBN-10: 0-7607-7518-4

Printed and bound in the United States of America

1 3 5 7 9 10 8 6 4 2

Contents

The Greatest

On September 5, 1960, a handsome young boxer from Louisville, Kentucky, stepped into the Olympic boxing ring in Rome, Italy. Muhammad Ali—known at the time as Cassius Clay—had bragged that he was "the greatest" since his very first boxing victory at age twelve. Now Clay was eighteen years old and a two-time winner of the amateur Golden Gloves tournament. He wanted desperately to defeat his opponent, the Polish boxer Zbigniew Pietrzykowski. If he beat Pietrzykowski, he would win the light-heavyweight gold medal.

Many sportswriters, however, were unimpressed with Clay's style. He did not fight like the large man he was. Instead of throwing powerful punches, he tended to rely on his legs. He danced quickly and gracefully around the ring to avoid being hit, while at the same time wearing out his opponent. "Clay had a skittering style, like a pebble scaled over water," wrote one well-known boxing critic. "He was good to watch, but he seemed to make only glancing contact."

Equally bad, in the eyes of these experts, were Clay's habits of holding his hands low, in a position that made him look vulnerable, and of leaning sideways to protect himself from punches. Clay ignored the criticism. He easily won his first three Olympic fights, all against stronger, heavier opponents.

The finals would be the toughest yet. Pietrzykowski, a three-time European champion and a 1956 bronze medalist, was a veteran of more than 200 fights. He had another advantage too: he fought left-handed, something that his young opponent did not handle well. Of the 108 bouts Clay had fought as an amateur, he had lost just eight times—but of those losses, two were to left-handed fighters.

The first round went badly for Clay. Pietrzykowski stood well back, out of Clay's range, yet managed to land blow after blow. At one point, Clay was so overwhelmed by a barrage of punches that he betrayed his inexperience by closing his eyes.

The second round went somewhat better for Clay. He managed to throw four hard rights to the head, but he was still losing on points. With Olympic boxing matches lasting only three rounds, Clay had to rally in the next round or lose the fight.

By the third round, the older fighter had begun to tire, and Clay came into his own. Instead of depending on his usual left jab, which was easily blocked by his left-handed opponent, Clay began to hit equally with his right. A series of combination punches left Pietrzykowski dazed. At the final bell, Pietrzykowski was slumped against the ropes, bleeding from cuts around his eyes, nose, and mouth. In contrast, Clay appeared as fresh "as if he had completed a few training press-ups," one journalist wrote. When the judges declared Clay the winner by unanimous decision, the crowd shouted its agreement.

The Cold War that was still simmering between the United States and the Soviet Union (USSR) made the victory even more significant for Clay. During the Cold War, which lasted from about 1945 to 1990, no direct military conflict occurred between the United States and the USSR. Yet suspicion, hostility, and mean-spirited competition were rampant on both sides. The Soviet Union had a Communist government and wanted more countries to become Communist. U.S. leaders saw Communism as a threat and wanted to stop its spread. In the 1960 Olympics, the USSR won more medals overall than the United States. Soviet leader Nikita Khrushchev gloated, "The triumph of the Soviet athletes is a victory for the man of the new socialist society."

Nonetheless, Clay had beaten fighters from the Soviet Union and Poland, both Communist countries. "I felt like I had defeated America's so-called enemies," he recalled later. Clay was so proud of his gold medal, he refused to take it off, even when he went to bed. He had to sleep on his back so the medal's sharp edges wouldn't cut into his skin.

The United States claimed to stand for freedom and equality, but in reality not all Americans were equal in 1960. As an African American, Clay was a second-class citizen, with or without a gold medal. Still, when a Soviet journalist asked him how it felt to represent a country where restaurants could refuse to serve him because of his skin color, Clay fired back, "To me, the USA is still the best country in the world, counting yours."

On his return to Louisville, Clay received a hero's welcome. For most athletes, winning an Olympic gold medal would be the absolute pinnacle of their achievements. Ali is one of the rare few who went on to achieve so much more that his gold medal has been nearly forgotten.

Chapter One

The Stolen Bicycle

Cassius Marcellus Clay Jr. was born in Louisville General Hospital at 6:35 P.M. on January 17, 1942. He was the first son of Odessa Grady Clay, a cook and housecleaner, and Cassius Marcellus Clay Sr., a sign painter and muralist. At his first weigh-in, the future champion was just 6 pounds, 7 ounces.

Cassius's unusual name had an equally unusual history. He had been named for Cassius Marcellus Clay, a farmer and slave owner before the Civil War (1861–1865) and one of the first people in Kentucky to free his slaves. Cassius's great-grandfather was brought up on Clay's property and, like many freed slaves, took the name of his white employer. The name had been passed down from father to son ever since.

According to family stories about Cassius, he was all but destined to become a famous boxer and entertainer. At six months old, one story goes, Odessa was cuddling Cassius when he stretched out an arm, hitting her hard in the mouth. Her front tooth was so loose afterward, it had to be removed. She later joked that it was Cassius's first knockout punch.

At ten months, Cassius started talking, "and once he started he always had something to say," Odessa recalled. The family nicknamed him "G. G." after his first babbling sounds, "gee gee gee gee." Once he became an amateur boxing champion, Cassius claimed he had been trying to say "Golden Gloves."

FRUSTRATED DREAMS

Although he was a sign painter by trade, Clay Sr. created religious murals for many of the Baptist churches in Louisville. He often told his sons that he would have liked to have been an artist. He was bitter that limited opportunities for African Americans prevented him from achieving his dreams.

Cassius's younger brother, Rudolph "Rudy" Valentino Clay, was born in 1944. The family lived in a small, four-room house at 3302 Grand Avenue in the West End, an all-black neighborhood. By the standards of the time, the family was middle class. Clay Sr. liked to brag that he was "never out of work for one day in my life and never worked for nobody but me." Sometimes Cassius and Rudy helped their father with his work. They learned how to mix paint, draw letters, and lay out a sign.

Louisville, often called the Gateway to the South, was a segregated city when Cassius was growing up. African Americans—then called "Negroes" or "colored"—were required to sit in the back of buses, drink from "colored" water fountains, and use "colored" restrooms. Only certain theaters, parks, and schools were open to African Americans.

According to one family story, young Cassius was out with his mother on a hot day, and he was thirsty. Odessa asked at a diner if she could have a drink for her son, but she was turned away. "I can only imagine the pain my mother felt," Clay wrote in his autobiography, *The Soul of a Butterfly*, "when she tried to find the words to explain why the man would not give me a glass of water."

Odessa, a devout Baptist, passed her deep faith on to both her sons. When Cassius was young, he would sneak outside in the dark and ask God what his purpose was in life. He later said, "I'd look at the stars and wait for a voice, but I never heard nothing."

But by age twelve, Cassius seemingly received his answer. That year his parents bought him an unusually expensive present. It was a brand-new red-and-white Schwinn bicycle. A few days later, Cassius and a friend rode their bikes to the Columbia

Auditorium to see the Louisville Home Show, an annual event featuring black-owned businesses. The two boys wandered happily through the auditorium, munching free popcorn and candy. When they decided to head home, they discovered that Cassius's new bike had been stolen.

❝I always felt like I was born to do something for my people.**❞**

—CASSIUS CLAY

Cassius was furious and soon began to cry. A sympathetic bystander suggested he report the theft to Joe Martin, a white police officer who coached boxing at the Columbia Gym in the building's basement. Cassius, still crying, told Martin exactly what he would do to the thief if he ever caught him. Martin heard him out, then told Cassius kindly that before he started making threats, he might want to learn how to fight.

The very next night, Cassius returned to the gym to begin his boxing training. He had found his purpose in life. He never did find the bicycle.

Chapter | Two

Tomorrow's Champion

Cassius enjoyed his boxing training from the beginning, but there was no indication he would ever be particularly good at it. "I guess I've taught a thousand boys to box, or at least tried to teach them," Joe Martin once said. "Cassius Clay, when he first began coming around, looked no better or worse than the majority."

Nonetheless, at twelve years old, Cassius was already on the way to becoming famous, at least in Louisville. As part of the Columbia Gym's amateur boxing program, Martin produced a local television show called *Tomorrow's Champions*. Just six weeks after beginning his training, Cassius made his first TV appearance in a fight against another young boxer, Ronnie O'Keefe. Cassius stood barely four feet tall and, like his opponent, weighed 89 pounds. During the three-minute, three-round bout, the two boys swung wildly at each other. Cassius landed a few more blows than Ronnie and was announced the winner by split decision. A split decision is when two of the three judges pick one boxer as the winner while one picks the other. When he heard he had won, Cassius shouted that he would soon be "the greatest of all time."

HOW TO WIN A BOXING MATCH

In modern amateur boxing, matches often have five judges. But in Clay's time, three judges scored amateur and professional matches. The judges awarded points to each fighter based on performance. The fighter with the most points was called the winner "by decision," which could either be "unanimous" (all three judges agree) or "split" (two of three agreed). A fighter could also win by "knockout" if his opponent fell to the floor and couldn't get up within ten seconds. In a "technical knockout" the referee stopped the bout because one of the fighters was too hurt to continue.

After just a year or two of training, Cassius began to show that he did indeed have some boxing potential. His speed made him stand out, as did his amazing reflexes. Very early, Cassius began to develop an unusual style of fighting. Boxers were supposed to hold their hands high to protect the head; Cassius held his very low, often below his waist. Boxers were supposed to duck or step aside to avoid punches; Cassius leaned away from blows, throwing himself off balance and leaving his chin open to a concealed punch. Only Clay's quickness and pinpoint timing allowed him the luxury of fighting his way. Most fighters who tried it would find themselves on the floor.

Cassius's uncanny ability to avoid being hit amazed boxing officials as well as his opponents. "Cassius would stand there, move his head two inches, turn his body another six inches, just slide over," recalled Bob Surkein, an Amateur Athletic Union (AAU) referee and judge. "I said to myself, it can't be"—but it was. When Cassius did get hit, he didn't panic like other amateurs or even some professionals. Instead, he recovered easily from the punch and went straight back to boxing.

❝ *You think he looks quick when you see him in his later fights, but that's slow compared to what he was as a young man. Slap, slap, slap, and gone.* ❞

—ANGELO DUNDEE, FUTURE TRAINER

Just as important as his natural gifts was his determination. Cassius began training like a professional while he was still a teenager. He woke between four and five in the morning to run several miles—what boxers call "roadwork"—before school. In

11

the afternoons, he worked out at the gym, staying long after the other boys had gone home for dinner. "It was almost impossible to discourage him," Martin recalled. "He was easily the hardest worker of any kid I ever taught." Cassius, who trained six days a week, also worked occasionally with an African American coach, Fred Stoner, at the Grace-Hope Community Center on the other side of town.

Cassius supplemented his demanding training schedule with a nutritional program of his own invention. For breakfast he had a quart of milk with two raw eggs in it. During the day, he sipped his own "health drink"—garlic water—claiming that soda pop was as deadly as cigarettes. At lunch he ate so much food, he needed two cafeteria trays to carry it all. Cassius's disciplined attitude brought quick results. In 1956, when he was fourteen years old, he won his first Golden Gloves title.

A year later, Cassius entered Louisville's main African American high school, Central High. The high school football coach wanted him to try out for the team, but Cassius turned him down because he considered football too dangerous. Cassius didn't want to risk any injuries that might prevent him from boxing.

Cassius had always struggled with reading and writing. He later concluded that he had dyslexia, a learning disability that makes reading and writing difficult. At the time, however, little was known about such disabilities, so Cassius received no extra help. "Back when I was in school, teachers figured that kids with learning difficulties were stupid," he recalled. With his boxing taking up so much time, Cassius let his schoolwork slide.

Meanwhile Cassius continued to excel in boxing. In 1958 he competed in the Golden Gloves Tournament of Champions in Chicago, Illinois. Here he suffered his first major loss when he was beaten by Tony Madigan, an Australian fighter and British Empire amateur champion. The following year, Cassius faced Madigan again at the Tournament of Champions, this time defeating him in a hard-fought, narrow victory. Cassius went on to win the 1959 National Golden Gloves title.

When Cassius was first competing as a boxer, the two major amateur competitions in the United States were the Golden Gloves tournament and the National AAU tournament. Amateur fights last for either three three-minute rounds or five two-minute rounds.

Cassius also won the 1959 National AAU Light-Heavyweight Championship. He then traveled to the University of Wisconsin for the finals of the Pan American Games trials. He lost to Amos Johnson on a split decision, breaking his streak of thirty-six consecutive wins. Johnson was much older, more experienced, and left-handed, but Cassius "didn't grumble or moan or complain," recalled Wilbert "Skeeter" McClure, another top amateur boxer at the time. "He just said like a champion, 'I couldn't figure him out.'"

In 1960 Clay won his sixth Kentucky Golden Gloves title, then returned to Chicago for his third Tournament of Champions. He temporarily fought as a heavyweight so that Rudy Clay, also an aspiring boxer, could compete in the light-heavyweight division without having to fight his older brother.

Even as an amateur, Cassius was a showman outside the ring. At the weigh-in for the 1960 Tournament of Champions, Cassius asked Martin casually if he were in a hurry to leave that evening. If so, he offered to knock out his opponent, Jimmy Jones—who was within hearing range, as Cassius intended—in one round. If not, Cassius said, he would take his time and fight all three rounds. Martin said he was in no hurry, so Cassius won the match in three rounds, as he had predicted. Martin didn't approve of such behavior. "I told him to cut that stuff out," he recalled later. "I told him, 'Anyone can talk big, let's see you hit big.' I might as well have been talking to a brick wall."

After winning the 1960 Tournament of Champions, Cassius traveled to New York to win his second national Golden Gloves title. In front of an audience of 15,000 people, he knocked out

Gary Jawish of Washington, D.C., who was 40 pounds heavier. Clay, who teetered on the brink between light-heavyweight and heavyweight, had been forced to load up on water before the weigh-in to meet the weight requirement. Also in 1960, Cassius successfully defended his AAU light-heavyweight title and was named the tournament's outstanding boxer.

In June 1960, eighteen-year-old Cassius graduated from high school—just barely. The stories vary, but according to one version, Cassius was failing English because his teacher had not allowed him to write a paper on the Nation of Islam (NOI). The NOI, a group also known as the Black Muslims, was based in Chicago. The teachings of the Nation of Islam are very different from those of traditional Islam. The group's leader, Elijah Muhammad, taught that the black race was God's favorite and that white people were evil. When Cassius had proposed to write a term paper on the group, his horrified teacher had forbidden it.

Cassius was saved when the principal of the school gave his legendary "Claim to Fame" speech. "One day our greatest claim to fame is going to be that we knew Cassius Clay, or taught him," he told the other teachers at a faculty meeting. "If every teacher here fails him, he's still not going to fail. . . . I'm going to say, *I taught him!*" Cassius was allowed to fulfill the term paper requirement by giving an oral presentation on the various cities he had visited as an amateur boxer. Ranked 376 out of a class of 391, he was given the lowest level of diploma, a "certificate of attendance."

Cassius's amateur boxing career stood in stark contrast to his academic one. Of 108 amateur matches, he had won an even 100, including six Kentucky Golden Gloves championships, two National Golden Gloves tournaments, and two National AAU titles. Cassius wanted to turn professional right away, but 1960 was an Olympic year. Martin persuaded him to try out for the Olympic boxing team instead. At the Olympic trials in San Francisco, California, Cassius defeated the U.S. Army champion, Allen Hudson, after the referee stopped the fight. Cassius had won the right to represent his country in the light-heavyweight division.

❝Even at eighteen, Clay was the most vivid, the most alive figure I'd ever met. You knew right away that you'd be hearing about him for years.❞
—DICK SCHAAP, NEWSWEEK SPORTS EDITOR

Unfortunately, Cassius had one small problem. He'd always been nervous about flying, and the flight to California had been particularly rough. He was terrified of the long flight over the

Atlantic Ocean to Rome—so terrified he said he wouldn't compete unless he could go by ship. Martin took Cassius to Louisville's Central Park and reasoned with him for hours until Cassius finally agreed to fly with the rest of the Olympic team.

Still nervous, Cassius came up with his own survival strategy. He went to an army surplus store and bought a parachute. "My plan was to drop to the floor as soon as the plane started shaking, with my parachute line ready in my hand, so I could jump out and pull the cord if our plane started to go down," he recalled. With the parachute strapped securely to his back, he talked as much as he could during the flight until finally he landed safely in Italy.

Chapter Three

Louisville Lip

Clay's Olympic gold medal was the last honor he would win as an amateur boxer. His plan was to begin fighting for prize money as soon as possible. "Right now," he told one reporter soon after the Olympics, "I'm amateur light heavyweight champion, and I'm broke."

Clay returned to Louisville and a blizzard of offers. Several colleges and universities contacted him about scholarships, but he rejected them. Instead, he focused on choosing a manager and a trainer from the dozens of people who wanted to handle him.

After negotiations with a few potential managers stalled, Clay signed a contract with the Louisville Sponsoring Group, a syndicate of eleven businessmen. Most were either millionaires or heirs to old Kentucky fortunes. The Louisville group had taken Clay on partly as an investment, partly for fun.

At the time, many boxers were managed by the Mafia—organized crime—or other questionable characters. Clay was lucky to sign with a group of solid businessmen who gave him an unusually fair contract, especially for an unknown fighter. He received a $10,000 signing bonus, a guaranteed salary of $4,000 a year, and 50 percent of any prize winnings. Knowing that boxers' careers were short, the syndicate also required that 15 percent of Clay's profits go into a pension fund, not to be touched until he was thirty-five or retired from boxing. As soon as he received his bonus, Clay celebrated by buying a pink 1959 Cadillac.

A LOST MEDAL?

According to one famous legend, shortly after Clay returned from Rome, he tried to order something to eat in a Louisville restaurant but was refused service because he was black. Clay was so angry, he threw his gold medal into the Ohio River. But in several interviews over the years, Clay has said that he simply lost the medal.

On October 29, 1960, three days after signing with the syndicate, Clay fought his first professional match in Louisville's Freedom Hall. His opponent was Tunney Hunsaker, a part-time fighter who was the full-time police chief of Fayetteville, West

Virginia. At twenty-nine, Hunsaker was an experienced fighter who had won fifteen of his twenty pro fights. Nonetheless, Clay was so relaxed before the bout, scheduled for 10:30 P.M., that at 9 P.M. he fell asleep in his dressing room. After Clay soundly defeated him in six rounds, Hunsaker made a prediction of his own: "He'll be heavyweight champion of the world someday."

Clay had worked with Fred Stoner, his old trainer, to prepare for his successful debut, but the Louisville Sponsoring Group wanted to find someone with more professional experience. In November Clay moved to Ramona, California, to train with Archie Moore, then the light-heavyweight champion of the world. Moore, an African American, was in his late forties—an old man by boxing standards—but still fighting.

The tough atmosphere at Moore's training camp, called the Salt Mine, appealed to Clay immediately. Scattered around the hilly camp were boulders with the names of great fighters painted on them. The gym, called the Bucket of Blood, was a big barn with a painting of a skull on the door.

Less appealing was Moore's disciplinarian streak. "He had all the natural talent in the world," Moore later said about Clay, "but he wasn't always willing to learn." Moore wanted to teach Clay to punch more powerfully so he could knock out an opponent in just one or two rounds. But Clay was proud of his unusual style—fast footwork and fast flurries of punches, like a featherweight in a heavyweight's body—and he resented Moore for trying to change it. Even more, Clay disliked having to wash dishes, mop floors, and do other chores, as Moore and all the other fighters did at the camp.

In December Clay quit training at the Salt Mine and returned to Louisville. Soon afterward the Louisville Sponsoring Group found him another trainer, Angelo Dundee. Dundee was based at the Fifth Street Gym in Miami, Florida.

Dundee, an Italian American, was one of the most respected trainers in boxing. His methods were as different from Moore's as could be imagined. Instead of bossing Clay around, Dundee made subtle suggestions. He complimented Clay on techniques he wasn't even using—such as turning his shoulder with a left hook—until Clay began to throw the punch that way, thinking it was his own idea. "Taught myself 98 percent of what I do," Clay told a reporter in 1961. "I just luck through with my own natural ability."

Ferdie Pacheco, the physician who worked with Dundee's fighters, was one of the few to pick up on Clay's less obvious advantages as a boxer. Clay's peripheral vision—his ability to see to his left and right while looking forward—was excellent, so he could track his opponents' every move. He could summon up enormous reserves of energy to survive long bouts. His bones were tough: no matter how powerful the punch, they didn't break. His skin was also tough, and his face was rounded, with no sharp edges where he could be cut easily. Clay's body seemed to be custom-made for fighting—"the most perfect physical specimen I had ever seen," Pacheco once said.

Dundee chose Clay's opponents carefully, wanting him to gain experience before he took on tougher fighters. While Clay racked up the wins, boxing writers remained skeptical about his talent. They liked his speed, but they questioned Clay's rule-breaking style. "He can fire blow after blow, but he does not yet have the big knockout punch that can explode with decisive force at any moment," wrote one well-known sportswriter. Clay was also criticized for throwing so many punches to his opponent's head rather than hitting the body, the conventional boxing strategy. "I'm a headhunter," Clay explained. "Keep punching at a man's head, and it mixes his mind."

U.S. sportswriters were just as skeptical about Clay's bragging outside the ring. At the time, sports stars—especially African American sports stars—were expected to be modest and polite. Clay was considered "uppity," which could be very dangerous for a black man in that era. During the first year of his professional career, the media invented a long list of semi-affectionate, semihostile nicknames for him. They included Gaseous Cassius, Claptrap Clay, Cash the Brash, Mighty Mouth, and, most famously, the Louisville Lip.

Clay loved meeting his fans and signing autographs. In Louisville he often visited his old elementary school and the Kosair Crippled Children Hospital, to which he donated his earnings from his pro debut.

In June 1961, Clay traveled to Las Vegas, Nevada, for his seventh professional fight, against the Hawaiian boxer Duke Sabedong. To promote the bout, Clay appeared on a local radio show with Gorgeous George, one of the most famous professional wrestlers of the time.

Compared to Gorgeous George, the Louisville Lip seemed almost humble. Gorgeous George threatened to kill his opponent and rip off his arm. If defeated, George promised, he would crawl across the ring and cut off his long golden hair. His act was so compelling, even Clay couldn't miss the fight. Clay discovered the arena was packed with spectators hoping to see Gorgeous George lose. "That's when I decided I'd never been shy about talking, but if I talked even more, there was no telling how much money people would pay to see me," he said later.

After meeting Gorgeous George (and defeating Sabedong by a ten-round decision), Clay's showmanship grew even more outrageous. It was no longer enough to claim to be the

"Greatest of All Time." He wrote poems describing his future victories and recited them for anyone who would listen. He bragged that despite his 108 amateur fights and growing number of professional fights, he was still "beautiful," an unusual description for a man, let alone a heavyweight boxer. "I'm too pretty to be a fighter," he boasted again and again. "Look at me—I'm as pretty as a girl." No serious athlete had ever behaved this way before. Reporters and sports fans simply did not know what to make of Clay's one-man circus.

❝[Clay's] loony goings-on have made him boxing's biggest draw outside of the heavyweight championship.**❞**

—DON MOSER, WRITER FOR LIFE MAGAZINE

Clay's most famous stunt—and the one that sold the most tickets to his fights—was to predict the exact round when he would knock out his opponent. He was usually right, though sometimes he had to work at it. Clay predicted a seventh-round victory over Willie Besmanoff, who was hopelessly outmatched. The fight, held in November 1961, lasted seven rounds only because Clay refused to knock Besmanoff out earlier. Against Don Warner in February 1962, Clay had predicted five rounds but ended up knocking him out in the fourth. Warner hadn't shaken hands before the fight, Clay explained afterward, so he had subtracted one round for poor sportsmanship.

Away from the spotlight and the microphone, Clay was often quiet, serious, philosophical, even shy. But whenever he had an audience, the Cassius Clay show was on. Only occasionally did he admit that his goofy behavior had a not-so-amusing explanation. "Where do you think I would be next week if I didn't know how to shout and holler and make the public sit up and take notice?" he told a reporter for *Sports Illustrated*. "I would be poor, for one thing, and I would be down in Louisville, my hometown, washing windows or running an elevator."

In late 1962, Clay signed a contract to fight Moore, his former trainer. At less than half his opponent's age and with a 15–0 record, Clay was heavily favored to win. Moore couldn't match Clay in the ring, but he was one of the few boxers who could keep up with his motormouth. During a mock debate held before the fight, Clay repeated his prediction poem: "When you come to the fight, don't block the aisle, and don't block the door. You will all go home after round four." Moore replied calmly, "The only way I'll fall in four, Cassius, is by tripping over your prostrate form."

In fact, Clay was easily able to fulfill his fourth-round prediction. Moore, known for his crablike crouching stance, bent lower and lower during the fight until he was practically doubled over. Clay hit one powerful left hook after another into the top of Moore's head until finally the fourth round arrived and he could knock Moore out. After the fight, Moore realized he hadn't needed to teach Clay to hit harder. "Clay throws punches so easily you don't realize how much they shock you until it's too late," he explained.

BLACK IS BEAUTIFUL

In the early 1960s, very few African American actors or fashion models were in the mainstream. The standard idea of "beauty" was based on white features. Many black Americans used chemicals to straighten their hair or even lighten their skin. For African Americans, Clay's declarations of his own attractiveness were powerful medicine. "Cassius Marcellus Clay . . . is a blast furnace of racial pride," stated a 1963 article in *Ebony* magazine.

In March 1963, Clay was booked to fight Doug Jones at Madison Square Garden in New York City. By then he had become a major celebrity. Seven of his previous eight fights had ended in the round he had predicted. His poetry was widely quoted in the media—*Life* magazine had even published an entire poem. But before the Jones fight, Clay faced a new public-relations problem. His fight coincided with a journalists' strike in New York. There were seven major newspapers in New York at the time, but not a single one was being published.

Clay set out to promote the fight any way he could—through television, radio, and mostly through personal appearances. He even read a poem about Jones during a poetry contest at the Bitter End, a hip Greenwich Village coffee shop. "This boy likes to mix, so he must fall in six," Clay told the room full of poetry fans before declaring himself "the Heavyweight Champion Poet of the World!" By the evening of the fight, Clay had revised his prediction to a fourth-round knockout, and Madison Square Garden was completely sold out.

Clay had repeatedly told reporters that he wasn't worried about Jones. He was simply one more opponent Clay had to knock out so that he could challenge Sonny Liston for the heavyweight championship of the world. "I'm not training too hard for this bum. Liston's the one I want," he told reporters. In the ring, Clay realized to his dismay that he had seriously underestimated his opponent, who was rated the number two world heavyweight contender by the World Boxing Association. The fourth round came and went, then the sixth, and Jones remained very much on his feet.

The fight ran the full ten rounds, and as it ended, many spectators thought Clay had lost. When Clay was announced the winner by decision, the furious crowd not only booed but pelted the ring with beer cups, cigar stubs, paper airplanes, and peanuts. Ever the showman, Clay picked up some of the peanuts, shelled them, and ate them.

After the fight, all reporters wanted to talk about was his inaccurate prediction. "First I called it in six," Clay told them. "Then I called it in four. Four and six, that's ten, right?" When reporters continued to heckle him, Clay made an uncharacteristic admission. "I ain't Superman," he said. "If the fans think I can do everything I say I can do, then they're crazier than I am."

Three months later, Clay had his first professional fight outside the United States. He traveled to London, England, to fight British heavyweight champion Henry Cooper.

Clay had predicted a fifth-round knockout, and by round three, it seemed like he could end the fight whenever he wanted. But each time Cooper looked ready to fall, Clay would back off and dance around the ring, determined to fulfill his fifth-round prediction.

By round four, Cooper had a cut above his left eye. Suddenly Cooper threw a left hook that caught Clay on the jaw, knocking him backward and through the ropes. Clay rolled back into the ring, but he seemed dazed. For the first time in his pro career, Clay was in real trouble. Suddenly the round ended; he had been saved by the bell.

Earlier in the fight, Dundee had noticed a small tear in one of Clay's gloves but had ignored it since the fight was going well. Now Dundee opened the tear a little more and told the referee, who tried to find a spare pair of gloves. In the time-out that followed, Dundee worked on Clay with cold sponges and smelling salts. No extra gloves were available, but the search had given Clay some precious time to recover.

By round five, the round he had predicted a win, Clay was ready. He hit Cooper in the face again and again. Cooper was bleeding so badly, spectators were shouting at the referee to stop the fight, and finally he did.

Afterward Clay told reporters he had left himself open to Cooper's big fourth-round punch because he had stared too long at the beautiful young actress Elizabeth Taylor, who had a ringside seat. He also celebrated with more boasting: "I'm not the greatest. I'm the double greatest. Not only do I knock 'em out, I pick the round. I'm the boldest, the prettiest, the most superior, most scientific, most skillfullest fighter in the ring today."

After the fight, Liston's manager, Jack Nilon, visited Clay in his dressing room. "I've flown three thousand miles to tell you we're ready," he said. Clay would finally have his chance to fight for the heavyweight championship of the world.

Chapter | Four

King of the World

In November 1963, Clay signed a contract to fight Sonny Liston for the heavyweight championship of the world. The physical fight against Liston was months away, but for Clay, the psychological one had already begun.

Clay's strategy against tough opponents was to undermine them in any way possible before the fight. His verbal abuse served a double purpose—to build interest in the bout and to confuse and anger his opponent. "I figured Liston would get so mad that, when the fight came, he'd try to kill me and forget everything he knew about boxing," Clay explained later.

Clay nicknamed Liston "the Bear" and taunted him about his alleged unattractiveness. "He's too ugly to be the world champ. The world's champ should be pretty like me," Clay told reporters. "I'm going to put that ugly bear on the floor, and after the fight I'm gonna build myself a pretty home and use him as a bearskin rug. Liston even smells like a bear. I'm gonna give him to the local zoo after I whup him."

Clay predicted he would knock Liston out in the eighth round and wrote a long poem describing it. In the verse, Clay hits Liston so hard, he lifts him clear out of the ring: "Now Liston disappears from view. / The crowd is getting frantic, / But our radar stations have picked him up. / He's somewhere over the Atlantic. / Who would have thought / When they came to the fight / That they'd witness the launching / Of a human satellite." Again and again, Clay described his fighting style in a slogan suggested by his assistant trainer, Bundini Brown: "Float like a butterfly, sting like a bee."

Clay was putting on a show, but most sportswriters and boxing fans didn't believe it. They thought his antics came out of deep fear of his famously tough opponent. Liston had learned to box in prison, where he had served time for armed robbery and assaulting a police officer. As a professional boxer, he was managed by the Mafia. Liston was thought to be unbeatable, perhaps even the greatest heavyweight of all time.

Liston's powerful punches were legendary. "Right hand destruction, left hand death," his manager once said. Liston usually defeated his opponents in the very early rounds. In 1962 he had won the heavyweight crown by knocking out the champion, Floyd Patterson, in just two minutes, six seconds. During the 1963 rematch, Patterson lasted four seconds longer: he hit the canvas in two minutes and ten.

Before the Liston fight, Clay was ranked the number one contender for the world title. Nonetheless, few boxing fans took him seriously. He had fought just nineteen professional bouts and had been knocked down twice by mediocre opponents. The odds were seven to one against Clay. Most people who bet on the fight didn't bother to bet on the winner but rather on the round that Liston would win.

Many boxing experts thought Liston might hurt Clay so badly, he would even end Clay's boxing career. Robert Lipsyte, the *New York Times* correspondent, was told by his editor to map out the route to the hospital so he could find it easily when Clay ended up there. One of the few who believed Clay could actually defeat Liston was Joe Martin, Clay's first trainer. "Clay can run faster backwards than Liston can forwards. It's as simple as that," Martin declared.

The buildup to the fight, scheduled for February 25, 1964, in Miami, Florida, was tremendous. But days before the bout, a storm of publicity about Clay's religious beliefs nearly caused the promoter to cancel it.

Clay was well known for being a reporter's best friend. He would talk to the press anytime, anywhere, and he nearly always said something worth quoting. But for several years,

Clay had been hiding a secret. He was becoming more and more involved with the Nation of Islam (NOI). Soon after moving to Miami, Clay had visited the local NOI temple, where he heard a sermon about the lost surnames of African slaves. While other races in the world had names that reflected their heritage, the speaker said, African Americans in the United States still bore the surnames of white slave owners. The sermon had a powerful effect on Clay. "It wasn't like church teaching, where I had to have faith that what the preacher was preaching was right," he said later. "And I said to myself, 'Cassius Marcellus Clay. He was a Kentucky white man, who owned my great-granddaddy and named my great-granddaddy after him. And then my grand-daddy got named, and then my daddy, and now it's me.'"

For the next three years, Clay attended the temple regularly, sneaking in through the back door to avoid being seen. At a time when race relations in the United States were at their most raw, the group's antiwhite message was dangerously controversial. Some people did not consider the Black Muslims to be a religious group at all, but rather a hate group like the Ku Klux Klan. Clay was afraid if news of his association with the Black Muslims leaked out, he would never be allowed to fight for the heavyweight championship.

Clay's secret first became known in September 1963, a few weeks before he signed to fight Liston. A Philadelphia paper reported that Clay had attended an NOI rally there. Remarkably, no other papers picked up the story—perhaps because they wrote it off as another of Clay's publicity stunts.

THE GREATEST

In 1963 Columbia Records released *The Greatest*, a spoken-word album of Clay's boxing monologues and poems. "Sonny Liston is nothing," Clay said on one track. "The man can't talk. The man can't fight. The man needs talking lessons. The man needs boxing lessons. And since he's gonna fight me, he needs falling lessons."

In January 1964, Clay gave a speech at a similar rally in New York. The result was a front-page news story. In the next few weeks, more papers—including the *Miami Herald*—published reports about Clay's relationship with the Black Muslims.

Bill MacDonald, the promoter of the Clay-Liston fight, was furious. In Florida segregation was still the law. MacDonald worried that no one would pay to see a fighter who believed white people were "blue-eyed devils," as Elijah Muhammad, the NOI's leader, called them. He threatened to cancel the fight unless Clay publicly renounced the group, but Clay refused. Reluctantly MacDonald agreed to let the fight continue.

The upcoming fight received massive international publicity, but only half of the eight thousand seats available at the Miami Convention Center had been sold. Few boxing fans wanted to pay the high ticket price when they expected Liston to knock out Clay in the first or second round. Once Clay's interest in the NOI became known, ticket sales slowed even more.

Even as Clay refused to answer questions about his involvement with the Nation of Islam, he continued to use publicity stunts to work on Liston's nerves. His final, notorious attempt came during the weigh-in before the fight.

Clay and his entourage entered the room first, chanting, "Float like a butterfly, sting like a bee. Your hands can't hit what your eyes can't see." When Liston walked in, Clay seemed to become almost hysterical. "I'm ready to rumble now!" he screamed. Clay tried to lunge at Liston but was held back by his trainer and two other members of his entourage. What few reporters noticed was that during the violent struggle, Clay winked at one of the men who was holding him back. The Miami Boxing Commission announced that Clay would be fined $2,500 for his disruptive behavior.

When the commission's doctor took Clay's blood pressure, he discovered it was dangerously high. Clay's pulse was more than double its normal rate. The doctor told reporters Clay was clearly emotionally unbalanced and terrified of his opponent.

Even journalists who had seen Clay's act many times before were confused, wondering if he really had lost control. On the way out of the room, Liston remarked to reporters, "You know, fellas, I don't think the kid's all there. I think he's scrambled in his marbles." That was exactly what Clay had hoped Liston would think. Liston later told reporter and former boxer José Torres that the only people he had feared in prison were those who were mentally ill—and now he thought Clay belonged to that group.

❝That's the only time I was ever scared in the ring. Sonny Liston. First time. First round. Said he was gonna kill me.❞

—Cassius Clay

After the weigh-in, reporters were even more certain that Liston would crush Clay. Wild rumors circulated. Clay had been seen at the airport trying to escape; the governor of Florida would cancel the fight because he didn't want blood on his hands. According to one poll, 93 percent of the accredited writers sent to Miami to cover the bout thought Clay would lose—assuming he even showed up. One reporter joked that Clay wouldn't make it through the national anthem.

Clay entered the ring wearing a white terry-cloth robe with The Lip stitched on the back. Liston followed, wearing his hood over his head like an executioner and with six rolled towels under his robe to make himself look bigger. Around the world, 750,000 fight fans tuned in via satellite transmission or closed-circuit broadcasts in movie theaters—a common way that important fights were shown then.

When the first-round bell rang, Clay bounded into the ring and began circling it, backpedaling, bobbing, weaving, ducking. Liston lunged with a left jab, missing by two feet. Again and again, Clay managed to slip Liston's punches. Each jab came just short of making contact. Liston had impressive reflexes himself, but he was no match for Clay. Later Clay said that he had managed to avoid punches by watching Liston's eyes. A certain small flicker tipped him off just before Liston was about to throw a powerful punch.

The first round ended, and, unlike Patterson and many other fighters who had challenged Liston before, Clay was still dancing. "I remember I got back to my corner thinking, 'He was supposed to kill me. Well, I'm still alive,'" Clay said later. Liston was so angry, he didn't even sit down.

The bell rang for round two, and Liston came out furiously, throwing big punches but missing badly. At one point, he managed to get Clay against the ropes, where he landed several hard body blows. This was the moment when boxing experts expected Clay to go down. Instead, Clay fought back, aiming at Liston's head, then slipped away and returned to circling the ring.

In round three, Clay changed his strategy. He had planned to coast until round five or six, then fight hard once Liston had begun to tire, but Liston was slowing down already. Clay hit Liston with a jab followed by a straight right, raising a welt on one side of his face and cutting the skin on the other—the first cut of Liston's professional career. After one combination of punches, Liston wobbled and nearly fell, but he managed to steady himself by holding on to the ropes.

Round four began more quietly. Clay went back to coasting, moving just enough to keep Liston hitting and missing. Liston, who was used to ending fights in the very early rounds, grew slower and slower. Suddenly Clay's eyes began to sting. An irritating substance had somehow gotten into them.

In the break between the fourth and fifth rounds, Angelo Dundee desperately tried to clean Clay's eyes, first with a towel, then a sponge. No one knew what the strange substance was. Liston's cornermen had treated his cut with medicine to stop the bleeding and his sore shoulder with liniment. Dundee guessed that one of these substances had gotten either onto Liston's gloves or Clay's gloves by accident. More skeptical observers, familiar with various ways to cheat in boxing, speculated later that an irritating substance was deliberately smeared on Liston's gloves. Either way, Clay was unable to see, and he panicked. He begged Dundee to cut his gloves off. Dundee refused. He sent Clay back into the ring with one instruction: "Run!"

Clay went into the fifth round blinking madly, able to see only the blurry outline of his terrifying opponent. Sensing his chance, Liston attacked, scoring several body shots and hooks to the face. Clay survived by dancing around the ring with his left arm stuck straight out, both to keep Liston away and to distract him. Liston was so tired that even with Clay half blind, he was unable to land a decisive punch.

❝ *That wasn't the guy I was supposed to fight. That guy could hit.* ❞

—SONNY LISTON

By round six, Clay's eyes had cleared, and he had caught a second wind. He fought flat-footed for nearly the entire round, the better to land powerful punches—left jabs, left hooks, combinations. For nearly three solid minutes, he attacked Liston, who seemed almost defenseless. At one point, Clay hit Liston with eight straight punches in a row until he doubled over. The crowd was in an uproar.

At the beginning of round seven, Clay bounced back into the ring, looking for his eighth-round knockout. Liston, still sitting on his stool in his corner, spat out his mouthpiece. (Boxers are required to wear protective mouthpieces throughout bouts.) Clay was one of the first to realize that Liston had given up. The heavyweight champion of the world had quit on his stool—something that hadn't occurred since 1919.

Clay raised both arms in the air and danced across the ring, his feet barely touching the canvas. "I am the greatest! I am the greatest! I am the greatest!" he shouted. "I'm the king of the world!" To the reporters, he shouted, "Eat your words! Eat! Eat your words!"

The Louisville Sponsoring Group had hoped only that Clay would survive the fight and had never even considered the possibility he might win. With no victory party planned, members of the group had to frantically arrange one at the last minute.

Clay decided not to attend his own party. Instead, he headed over to the motel where his close friend Malcolm X was staying with his family. Born Malcolm Little, he had joined the NOI while in prison for robbery and had changed his last name to X to represent his lost African name. Soon after he and Clay met in Detroit in 1962, he became Clay's trusted spiritual adviser.

MALCOLM X

Malcolm X was the Nation of Islam's most famous spokesperson. But later in 1964, Malcolm X renounced his antiwhite beliefs and broke with the Nation of Islam to set up his own organization. Soon afterward he was assassinated by NOI thugs. *The Autobiography of Malcolm X*, cowritten with Alex Haley, was published after his death.

The new heavyweight champion of the world, who had turned twenty-two just a few weeks before, celebrated his upset victory by eating an enormous dish of vanilla ice cream. After a short nap on Malcolm X's bed, he went home.

Chapter Five

Black Muslim

C lay had amazed even the most hardened boxing reporters with his bizarre behavior at the weigh-in, followed by his defeat of a supposedly unbeatable opponent. But Clay was not yet out of surprises.

At the press conference the next morning, Clay was subdued and soft-spoken. There were no poems, no monologues, no name-calling. With the microphone system in the room not working, journalists had to ask the famously loudmouthed Clay to speak up. Clay gave the reporters simple, almost dull answers to their questions. He was happy to be champion, he wasn't surprised he had won, and he had defeated Liston simply because he was the better fighter. Then one journalist asked, "Are you a card-carrying member of the Black Muslims?"

"Card-carrying, what does that mean?" Clay answered. "I believe in Allah and in peace. I don't try to move into white neighborhoods. I don't want to marry a white woman. I was baptized when I was twelve, but I didn't know what I was doing. I'm not a Christian anymore. I know where I'm going and I know the truth, and I don't have to be what you want me to be. I'm free to be what I want."

NATION OF ISLAM BELIEFS

The Nation of Islam was founded by W. D. Fard in Detroit in 1930. According to Fard, seventy-six trillion years ago, a black man, the "Original Man" now known as Allah, created the known universe and then the black race. Later an evil scientist, Yacub, created the white race by mating lighter-skinned men and women. Whites were banished to Europe, where they lived like animals.

Cleanliness and discipline were important values for NOI followers. They were not allowed to smoke, drink, or eat pork. Interracial marriage was banned, as were homosexuality and adultery. Women were encouraged to cover their hair and wear ankle-length dresses.

The reaction to Clay's announcement was almost uniformly hostile. He had outraged nearly everyone, from white racists to civil rights leaders. The U.S. Senate threatened to investigate the legality of the Liston fight. The World Boxing Association tried to strip him of his title for "conduct detrimental to the best interests of boxing." Television appearances were canceled, endorsement deals evaporated, and his spoken-word album was withdrawn. The Louisville Sponsoring Group publicly called Clay "ungrateful." Even Martin Luther King Jr. joined in the criticism: "When Cassius joined the Black Muslims," he said in a sermon, "he became a champion of racial segregation and that is what we are fighting against."

One of Clay's few supporters was African American baseball star Jackie Robinson. Ignoring the Nation of Islam's racist views, Robinson wrote in an influential black newspaper, "Clay has just as much right to ally himself with the Muslim religion as anyone else has to be a Protestant or a Catholic."

At first Clay took the name "Cassius X Clay." Most members of the Nation used X as a last name. NOI's leader, Elijah Muhammad, rewarded loyal, longtime believers with so-called original names. Breaking with tradition, just a few weeks after Clay's public announcement, Elijah Muhammad gave him an original name, Muhammad Ali.

In Arabic, *Muhammad* means "worthy of all praises," while *Ali* means "most high." "Changing my name was one of the most important things that happened to me in my life," Ali once said. "It freed me from the identity given to my family by slave masters." But many reporters and editors continued to refer to him as "Cassius Clay" for years afterward.

 Ali's younger brother, Rudy, joined the NOI before Cassius did. Later Rudy was given the name Rahaman Ali.

In May 1964, Ali took a monthlong tour of Africa—partly as a spiritual voyage, partly to escape the nonstop negative publicity. He traveled first to Ghana, where he was received like a conquering hero. He received similar treatment in Egypt. One of Ali's companions on the Africa trip was Herbert Muhammad, the third of Elijah Muhammad's six sons. When Ali returned from Africa, he traveled to Chicago, where Herbert Muhammad introduced him to a young woman named Sonji Roi.

At twenty-three, Roi was a year older than Ali. Strikingly beautiful, she supported herself by working as a cocktail waitress and photographer's model. Roi wasn't a Muslim, and in many ways, her lifestyle conflicted with Muslim beliefs. Nonetheless, Ali was immediately smitten. On the night of their first date, he asked Roi to become his wife.

Three weeks later, Ali and Roi were married in Islamic fashion. A member of the Nation of Islam performed a wedding ceremony in front of two witnesses. They were married legally by a justice of the peace in Gary, Indiana, on August 14, 1964. Roi promised Ali she would adhere to the strict Islamic standards for women. But she chose to take his discarded surname, becoming Sonji Clay.

TOLERANCE AND INTOLERANCE

Even as he publicly professed a radical religion, Ali was surrounded by people who were white and of other faiths. His trainer, Angelo Dundee, was Italian American; his assistant trainer, Bundini Brown, was African American and Jewish; Ferdie Pacheco, his doctor, was Cuban; Howard Bingham, his closest friend, was African American and Christian.

It had been a tumultuous six months for Ali. He had a new title, a new name, and now a new wife. His physical condition had suffered. For the first time, his weight had ballooned to 231 pounds. It was time to rededicate himself to boxing. Soon after his marriage, Ali returned to Miami to begin serious training for his rematch with Sonny Liston.

Chapter Six

Unbeatable

Ali's rematch against Sonny Liston was scheduled for November 16, 1964, at Boston Garden. Ali never doubted that he could repeat his victory over Liston, but boxing experts remained deeply skeptical. The fact that Liston had simply quit on his stool tarnished the victory. True, Ali had survived, but had he really won?

Once again, Liston was favored, though this time by much smaller odds. Back to his usual self-promotion tricks, Ali predicted a ninth-round knockout, then cut it to three. "Only fools believe I beat him by accident last time," he told reporters.

Before their first fight, Liston had underestimated Ali and had not taken his training seriously. This time he trained with dedication bordering on fury. He ran five miles a day in hilly country and worked out with a martial arts instructor to improve his agility. Ali trained equally hard. He quickly lost the weight he had gained on his trip to Africa. Although he was back down to 210 pounds, he had grown as a fighter, with more muscular arms and legs.

Ali seemed to be in supreme condition. But on the evening of November 13—just three days before the fight—he suddenly became violently ill. Ali's brother offered to call a doctor so the press wouldn't find out, but Ali was in such intense pain, he insisted on going to a hospital.

The doctors discovered Ali had an incarcerated inguinal hernia—a swelling the size of an egg in his abdomen—that required immediate surgery. The potential to develop the hernia had been inherited and wasn't caused or worsened by Ali's boxing. Nonetheless, doctors said later that if Ali had entered the ring with this condition, he might have died. The Liston fight was postponed for six months to give Ali time to recover.

On May 25, 1965, in Lewiston, Maine, Ali and Liston finally fought their long-awaited rematch. The international television and closed-circuit audience was huge. For the first time, a heavyweight title fight would be seen in Africa and the Soviet Union.

Clay was loudly booed as he entered the ring and booed again as he was introduced. In a fight against an avowed Black Muslim, ex-convict Liston had become the unlikely popular favorite. At the opening bell, Ali rushed across the ring and surprised Liston with a hard right. Then he began to dance, holding his gloves low, as Liston plodded after him. For twenty seconds, the fighters circled each other without either one attempting to throw a punch.

Liston fired four lefts, which all landed but glancingly, muffled by Ali's gloves and forearms. He tried to jab but couldn't hit Ali cleanly. About a minute into the fight, Ali landed a second punch, another right that stunned his opponent.

Then came the crucial moment of the bout. Liston lunged forward with a left jab. Ali pulled his chin back to avoid being hit and, pivoting forward, counterpunched with a powerful straight right that landed on Liston's temple.

❝ *In boxing, the punch that knocks you out is not the hard punch. It's the punch you don't see coming. And Ali was a master at that.* ❞
—José Torres, light-heavyweight champion in 1965 and author of *Sting Like a Bee: The Muhammad Ali Story*

The punch was so incredibly quick that many fans, even those seated at ringside, didn't see it. The combined speed and accuracy of the blow lifted Liston's left foot—where he had most of his weight—off the canvas. Knocked off balance, Liston sank to his knees, then his elbow, and finally rolled onto his back. Ali tried to follow up with a left hook as Liston fell but missed. Liston was already too near the floor.

According to the rules of boxing, when one fighter is knocked down, the other is required to retreat to a neutral corner. But Ali remained in the center. As cries of, "Fake! Fake!" arose from the crowd, Ali stood over Liston, shouting at him: "Get up and fight, you bum! You're supposed to be so bad! Nobody will believe this!"

The referee, who said later he was afraid Ali would kick Liston in the head, tried to shove Ali to a neutral corner so he could begin the count. After ten seconds, the official timekeeper shouted that Liston had been down for the count of ten—a knockout—but the referee didn't hear him. When Liston finally struggled to his feet, he had been lying on the canvas for seventeen seconds. Nonetheless, the referee, who had lost track of the count, called the fighters to resume. Ali charged back, throwing punches. Only when Nat Fleischer, the publisher of *Ring* magazine, began shouting the referee's name and, "It's over! He's out!" did the referee stop the fight. Ali, who had landed just three punches during the entire match, was ruled the winner by knockout.

The crowd roared in anger and disbelief. Canadian heavyweight champion George Chuvalo, who had planned to fight Liston if he won, leapt through ropes, grabbed Ali's arm, and shouted, "Fix! Fix!" Even Ali wasn't sure he had actually knocked Liston down until he watched the footage of his own punch in slow motion. To skeptical reporters who said they had missed the so-called phantom punch, Ali said, "Don't feel bad. Sonny was closer and he didn't see it either."

The huge international audience had witnessed one of the shortest fights in heavyweight championship history—less than two minutes long. Afterward there were stories of unfortunate fans at theaters who had stopped to buy popcorn and missed the entire fight. The "phantom punch" did little to enhance Ali's reputation as a fighter or his public image. In the days after the bout, Ali told reporters that the knockout blow had been his "secret anchor punch." He claimed he had learned it from a close friend, the elderly comedian Stepin Fetchit. Fetchit, he said, had learned it from the first-ever black heavyweight champion, Jack Johnson. Fleischer, *Ring*'s publisher, thoroughly researched Ali's claim but said later that Johnson had never had such a punch.

Ali was at the peak of his professional career, but his personal life was troubled. A month after the Liston fight and less than a year after his marriage, Ali filed for an annulment (a legal term that means a marriage was never valid). Ali claimed that Sonji had not followed the beliefs of his Muslim religion as she had promised to do. Sonji disputed the claim, saying that she merely asked too many questions about the Black Muslims, raising contradictions that Ali couldn't answer.

❝ *I had to prove you could be a new kind of black man. I had to show that to the world.* **❞**

—MUHAMMAD ALI

Meanwhile Ali began training for his next fight, against former world champion Floyd Patterson. In many respects, Patterson was the opposite of Ali. He was soft-spoken, humble, and popular with both the press and boxing fans—especially white fans. After the two first-round knockouts he suffered at the hands of Liston, Patterson had come back to win five consecutive fights. Patterson, who had been the youngest heavyweight champion in history, was also the only fighter to have won the title twice. Now he wanted to try to win it a third time.

At first Ali promoted the fight in his usual joking style. He nicknamed Patterson "the Rabbit," an animal he said was scared of its own shadow. In a typical publicity stunt, he turned up at Patterson's training camp with two heads of lettuce and a bunch of carrots.

Unexpectedly, Patterson retaliated with ugly rhetoric. In an article for *Sports Illustrated*, Patterson wrote that he intended to "reclaim the title for America"—as if a foreigner had won it. "No decent person can look up to a champion whose credo is 'hate whites,'" wrote Patterson. "The image of a Black Muslim as the world heavyweight champion disgraces the sport and the nation." Patterson even offered to fight Ali for free.

Ali reacted with insults of his own. He attacked Patterson for trying to move into an all-white neighborhood and called him an "Uncle Tom"—a black person who would do anything to win whites' approval. Never had two African American athletes poured so much racial scorn and abuse on each other.

The fight was held in Las Vegas on November 22, 1965. From the opening bell, it was clear that Patterson was no match for Ali, who didn't even bother to throw a punch during the first round. During the fight, Ali taunted Patterson again and again with racial insults.

Early in the fight, Patterson suffered a painful muscle spasm in his back—a problem that had troubled him for years. By the fifth round, Patterson was finding it difficult even to walk, but he refused to quit. Ali hit Patterson nineteen times in the face before pausing to catch his breath. Then he hit him with four more jabs before the bell rang.

Midway through the fight, Patterson's legs were wobbly, and Ali knocked him down with his trademark left jab. It was clear that Ali could end the fight whenever he wanted. But each time Patterson looked ready to collapse, Ali would give him time to recover. Finally, in round twelve, the referee stopped the fight. When Ali was announced the winner by technical knock-out, the crowd booed Ali and cheered Patterson.

After his victory, the media hated Ali even more than before. Even publications that had previously run positive stories turned against him. *Life* magazine was one. *Life*'s coverage of the fight was headlined "Sickening Spectacle in a Ring." Robert Lipsyte of the *New York Times* compared Ali's torture of Patterson to a little boy pulling the wings off a butterfly.

On January 10, 1966, Ali's marriage to Sonji ended. Sonji said later that she was sure that the Nation of Islam had pressured Ali to leave her and that it had not been his own decision. For years afterward, when sportswriters asked Ali which of his opponents had been the toughest, he would invariably answer, "My first wife."

Chapter Seven

Champion in Exile

Meanwhile in 1965, the United States began bombing North Vietnam. The roots of the Vietnam conflict went back decades and had to do with the U.S. desire to halt the spread of Communism. The United States was trying to prop up the government of South Vietnam in its war against North Vietnam, which was controlled by the Communist Vietcong.

At first many Americans supported the war, even when young men began to be drafted (required to serve in the military). As a healthy U.S. male in his early twenties, Ali seemed like a prime candidate for the draft.

Earlier he had been ordered to take the military qualifying examination. Ali aced the physical tests but struggled to complete the written exam, especially the math section. "When I looked at a lot of the questions they had on them army tests, I just didn't know the answers," he said later. "I didn't even know how to start after finding the answers." His IQ was calculated at 78. (A score of 100 indicates average intelligence.) Ali had failed the exam.

Ali was later tested again to make sure he hadn't deliberately failed. Three army psychologists supervised the exam, and once again he didn't pass. Ali was classified 1-Y, "not qualified under current standards for service in the armed forces." When the media picked up the story—and his poor high school record was made public—Ali was embarrassed. "I said I was the greatest, not the smartest," he told reporters.

HATE MAIL

During the years when Ali was classified 1-Y, the Louisville draft board received more than 1,000 letters from all over the country demanding that Ali be sent to Vietnam. Most were full of racial hatred. A typical example: "When are you going to have the guts to . . . put him in the Army where we all hope he'll have his head shot off?"

In early 1966, as the war in Vietnam escalated, the military was forced to lower its standards. In February Ali was reclassified 1-A, available for the draft. Ali was upset and confused. He knew little about politics and could not even locate Vietnam on a map. After a day of answering journalists' questions, all the while growing more and more agitated, Ali finally exploded. "I ain't got no quarrel with them Vietcong," he said.

Once again Ali was front-page news. At a time when most Americans considered the Vietcong the enemy, Ali's remark was seen as deeply offensive and unpatriotic. The well-connected Louisville Sponsoring Group offered to help Ali find less dangerous ways to serve. He could join the reserves, the National Guard, or the Special Services, performing exhibition matches to entertain the troops. Many young men, white or black, would have happily accepted such an easy way out, but Ali would not. In March 1966, one month after being reclassified 1-A, Ali appeared before the draft board to declare himself a conscientious objector—someone who could not serve in the military because of his personal beliefs.

Ali's next fight, against Ernie Terrell in Chicago, had also been scheduled for March 1966. But after his Vietcong remark, the *Chicago Tribune*—followed by newspapers across the country—called on the Illinois State Athletic Commission to ban the match. Without waiting for the commission's decision, the governor of Illinois took back the license for the fight.

The promoters tried to move the bout elsewhere. Louisville was considered, but then the Kentucky State Legislature passed a resolution condemning Ali. After running into similar hostility in other American cities, the promoters had to stage the fight in Toronto, Canada. When many closed-circuit theaters decided not to show the bout, Terrell pulled out as well. Ali had to fight Canadian heavyweight champion George Chuvalo, and still the American press called for a boycott.

Ali ignored the public criticism as best he could and tried to promote the fight in his usual way. At first Ali nicknamed Chuvalo "the washerwoman," though after he watched Chuvalo train, he was impressed enough to change it to "washerman." Chuvalo was a tough opponent, with impressive stamina, and had never been knocked out. The fight lasted the full fifteen rounds—the longest fight of Ali's career so far—during which Chuvalo landed many hard body shots. Nonetheless, Ali was announced the winner by unanimous decision.

From 1966 to 1967, Ali successfully defended his title seven times. Since political pressure made it difficult for him in the United States, he fought overseas. In May 1966, Ali had a rematch with Henry Cooper in London, defeating him in the sixth round. In August Ali fought another British boxer, Brian London, knocking him out in the third. In September he traveled to Frankfurt, West Germany, where he took twelve rounds to defeat Karl Mildenberger, a tricky left-handed opponent. The Mildenberger fight marked the last time an Ali fight would be shown on U.S. television for seven years.

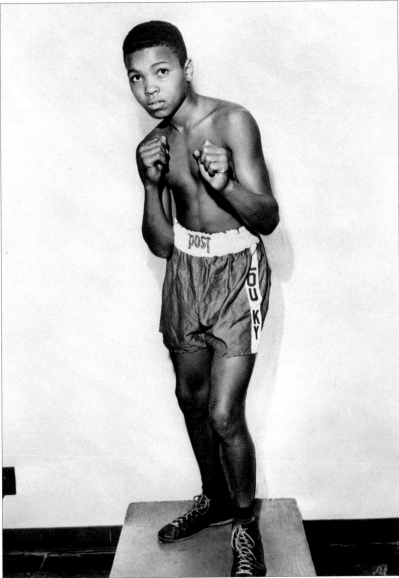

At age twelve, Muhammad Ali was known as Cassius Clay, and he was just learning the basics of boxing.

In 1960 Cassius Clay won a gold medal at the Olympic Games in Rome, Italy. He stands with silver medalist Zbigniew Pietrzykowski *(right)* and bronze medalists Giulio Saraudi *(left)* and Anthony Madigan *(far left)*.

Cassius Clay celebrates after his 1963 victory over Henry Cooper in London, England. It was Clay's nineteenth professional fight and his first fight outside the United States.

As Clay became involved with the Nation of Islam (NOI) in the early 1960s, he developed a close friendship with Malcolm X *(right, with camera)*. In mid-1964, NOI leader Elijah Muhammad gave Clay a new name: Muhammad Ali.

Muhammad Ali fought Sonny Liston for the second time on May 25, 1965. After delivering a knockout punch in the first round, Ali taunted Liston, telling him to keep fighting.

Ali blocks punches from George Foreman *(right)*. This 1974 matchup took place in Kinshasa, Zaire (later renamed the Democratic Republic of the Congo), and Ali nicknamed it the "Rumble in the Jungle." Ali knocked out Foreman in the eighth round to become heavyweight champion of the world for the second time.

Muhammad Ali returned to the Olympic Games in 1996 to light the torch at the opening ceremony in Atlanta, Georgia.

In November 2005, the Muhammad Ali Center opened in Louisville, Kentucky. Ali's family, including daughters Jamillah *(far left)* and Rasheda *(left),* and his wife, Lonnie *(right),* joined him to celebrate the opening weekend.

Meanwhile, in the fall of 1966, Ali's contract with the Louisville Sponsoring Group had expired, and Ali decided not to renew it. His new manager was Elijah Muhammad's son Herbert Muhammad—a close spiritual adviser and the man who had introduced Ali to his first wife. The media saw this as one more sign that Ali was rejecting white society.

❝*Muhammad Ali is a genius. He has a power that great fighters never had. Don't watch Ali's gloves, arms, or legs when he's fighting. Watch his brains.*❞

—JOSÉ TORRES

Soon afterward Ali's promoters finally managed to schedule two fights for him in the United States: Cleveland Williams in November 1966 and Ernie Terrell in February 1967. Both took place in Houston, Texas. Even in such a politically charged atmosphere, Ali didn't abandon his lighthearted promotional tactics. He promised that during the Williams fight, he would unveil a new dance step, the "Ali shuffle," that would sweep the nation. The shuffle turned out to be a quick crisscross of legs, intended to distract his opponent; sometimes he would throw a punch while he was dancing. Ali easily knocked out Williams in three rounds.

The Terrell fight was different. Before the bout, Terrell had called Ali "Clay"—at first by accident, then deliberately. The fight was brutal and ugly; Ali kept shouting, "What's my name?" as he hit Terrell again and again. Afterward Terrell claimed Ali had deliberately stuck a finger in his eye, though Ali denied it. As he had when he fought Patterson, Ali dragged the fight out as long as possible, to the full fifteen rounds. The press and the public were appalled that Ali would torture an opponent so cruelly while claiming conscientious objector status. An Illinois congressman observed in the U.S. House of Representatives, "Apparently Cassius will fight anyone but the Vietcong."

On March 22, 1967, Ali fought Zora Folley in New York's Madison Square Garden. Ali knocked down Folley in the fourth round. Ali raised his arms in victory, only to find Folley had struggled to his feet. In the seventh round, Ali finally knocked Folley out with another "phantom punch"—so swift that many spectators missed it. Angelo Dundee, Ali's trainer, later said the fight had been Ali's best. It was also his last fight of the 1960s.

Ali's date for induction into the military was set for April 28, 1967, in Houston, Texas. The induction ceremony was very simple. An officer slowly read aloud a list of names. Each young man, when he heard his name, took one step forward. When Ali's legal name was read—Cassius Marcellus Clay—he remained absolutely still.

Ali was taken out of the room and reminded that refusing induction was a felony. He was brought back to the ceremony room, and his name read once more. Again Ali remained motionless. He was then asked for a written statement. "I refuse to be inducted into the armed forces of the United States," Ali wrote, "because I claim to be exempt as a minister of the religion of Islam."

Ali had finally pushed the establishment too far. An hour after he had refused induction—before he had been charged, let alone convicted, with any crime—the New York State Athletic Commission suspended his boxing license and withdrew recognition of him as world champion. Almost immediately the other states in the country followed suit. Ali's beloved heavyweight title, which he had earned and defended in the ring, was gone.

In June 1967, Ali was tried and found guilty of refusing induction into the military. The judge imposed the maximum sentence allowable—five years' imprisonment and a fine of $10,000. Ali remained free on appeal, but his passport was taken away. Since he had already been banned from fighting in the United States—not even an exhibition match was allowed—the passport decision destroyed his boxing career.

To many people in the African American community, Ali's stand made him a hero. More young black men were being drafted than white men, and Ali was one of the few to have the bravery to resist. "No matter what you think of Muhammad Ali's religion," Martin Luther King Jr. said in one of his sermons, "you certainly have to admire his courage." Howard Cosell, a Jewish sportscaster, was one of the few people in the world of sports to defend Ali's right to refuse to serve in the military.

THE NEW CHAMPION

After Ali's heavyweight championship title was taken away, an eight-man elimination tournament was held to determine the new heavyweight champion. The winner was Jimmy Ellis, a Louisville boxer who as a young man had trained with Ali at Joe Martin's gym. During his exile from boxing, Ali thought of himself as the "People's Champion."

On August 17, 1967, Ali married for the second time. Belinda Boyd, an employee at one of the businesses owned by the NOI, had been raised a Black Muslim and was deeply religious. She was just seventeen years old. Ten months after their marriage, Belinda gave birth to a daughter, Maryum. The couple later had twin daughters, Rasheda and Jamillah, and a son, Muhammad Jr.

Ali had trained in just one profession, boxing. With no way to support his growing family, he fell back on his second-greatest talent: speaking. He signed a contract with a professional speakers' bureau and began to lecture at colleges across the nation. During his lectures, Ali spoke about his political and religious beliefs and read his poetry.

In addition to lecturing, Ali pursued various other entertainment ventures. He was paid to appear in a documentary about him, *A/K/A Cassius Clay*. He fought a mock boxing match with former heavyweight champion Rocky Marciano, with the winner determined by computer analysis of various boxing statistics. He even starred in a Broadway musical, *Buck White*. The play was short-lived, but Ali's acting and singing skills impressed some tough New York theater critics.

Chapter Eight

The Champion Returns

For three and a half years, Ali was completely locked out of professional boxing. Even when Ali tried to fight an exhibition match for charity, he couldn't get a license.

During his years in exile, Ali's antiwar position never wavered, but the rest of the United States underwent a dramatic political shift. By 1970 public opinion had turned against the war—and, remarkably, in favor of Ali. To the black community and to young people, Ali had long been a symbol of resistance. Many mainstream Americans came to share their view. Ali wasn't a draft dodger but a hero who had sacrificed his career, his title, and millions of dollars for his beliefs.

Suddenly, after years of failure, Ali's promoters found a U.S. city that would host a fight—Atlanta, Georgia. Georgia had no athletic commission; boxing matches in Atlanta required only the mayor's permission. Under pressure from Atlanta's powerful African American community, the mayor reluctantly agreed to allow the fight.

Ali was originally scheduled to fight then-heavyweight champion Joe Frazier. Frazier beat Ellis in February 1970 to claim the title, but he knew he would never really be considered champion until he defeated Ali.

When Frazier pulled out over a scheduling conflict, however, the promoters had to find a new opponent. Jerry Quarry, an Irish American, was the number-one contender for the title and, like Frazier, a hard puncher. A reporter had once compared a Frazier-Quarry fight to two Mack trucks meeting in a narrow street.

The Ali-Quarry fight was scheduled for October 26, 1970. Beforehand Ali received numerous death threats. Wild rumors said that the match would be canceled by Georgia's prosegrega-tion governor, Lester Maddox, or by interventions from the Ku Klux Klan or veterans' groups.

Before the match, Ali didn't offer his usual prediction of the knockout round. He barely dared to speak publicly, fearing the bout would be canceled at the last minute: "I'll believe I have a fight when I'm in the ring and I hear the bell."

The crowd was overwhelmingly African American and overwhelmingly behind Ali. Coretta Scott King, the widow of Martin Luther King Jr., was there, as were civil rights leader Jesse

Jackson, comedian Bill Cosby, and singer Diana Ross. Few were boxing fans. They hadn't come to see a boxing match but the return of their hero. When the boxers were announced, Quarry received a solid round of applause, but the crowd screamed so loudly for Ali that his name couldn't be heard above the roar.

In the first round, Ali came out powerfully, as if he were throwing all the punches he hadn't been allowed to throw over the last three years. But in the second round Ali slowed down noticeably. Quarry landed several hard punches to Ali's head, then backed him up against the ropes and pummeled his body. The few boxing experts in the crowd were surprised and confused.

> The number of rounds in a professional boxing match varies. Fights may be as short as four rounds. When Ali first turned pro, championship fights were fifteen rounds. To cut down on injuries, championship fights became twelve rounds in the 1980s.

By round three, Quarry was gaining confidence. The situation seemed grim for Ali. Suddenly Ali opened an enormous cut over Quarry's eye, despite the grease Quarry had applied to his face to prevent it. Quarry wanted to fight on, but his trainer told the referee to stop the fight. Furious, Quarry burst into tears.

Ali had won, delighting the crowd of nonboxing fans. But to boxing experts, he wasn't the same Ali they had last seen in 1967. He had become much slower, without the same split-second timing. His primary defense had always been his legs, and now they seemed to be failing him.

Even more worrisome was Ali's new habit of leaning against the ropes. Traditionally, the ropes are a sort of halfway point between standing up and lying on the canvas—a place where a boxer stops to try to recover. Ali seemed to be depending on the ropes to compensate for his loss of speed.

Nonetheless, Ali was determined to win his championship back. His next fight, just over a month later, was in New York. Earlier the National Association for the Advancement of Colored People (NAACP) Legal Defense Fund had sued the state of New York on Ali's behalf. One astonishing piece of evidence was a list of ninety felons who had been licensed to fight there. In overturning the New York State Athletic Commission's decision to ban Ali, the judge called it "intentional, arbitrary, and unreasonable discrimination."

On December 7, 1970, Ali made his triumphant return to New York's Madison Square Garden. His opponent was Oscar Bonavena, an Argentinean boxer whom one writer called "indestructible." Bonavena threw painfully hard blows, yet bounced back from his opponents' attacks "as if he were a heavy bag."

Ali, who had predicted a ninth-round knockout, was favored to win by six-to-one odds. In the early rounds, Ali was in complete control of the fight. By round five, Ali was beginning to tire and had retreated to the ropes, where Bonavena pounded him again and again. Ali fought hard in the ninth round, trying to end it as he had predicted, but Bonavena wouldn't let him. The fight dragged on until the fifteenth round, when Ali knocked Bonavena down three times, winning the fight by technical knockout.

Despite his mediocre performances against Quarry and Bonavena, Ali wanted to challenge Frazier for the heavyweight title as soon as possible. Pacheco, Ali's physician, wanted Ali to take time to train and recover from the beating he received from Bonavena. But with Ali's appeals still pending, it was unclear how much time he had—or if he would soon be sent to jail.

On March 8, 1971, Ali finally would have his chance to fight for the heavyweight title. For the first time, two undefeated heavyweight champions—each with a legitimate claim to the title—would battle to determine its rightful owner. Ali and Frazier would each earn a record $2.5 million, an enormous sum at the time.

Frazier, a gold medalist at the 1964 Tokyo Olympics in Japan, was a formidable opponent. Undefeated for six years, he had scored twenty-three knockouts in twenty-six fights. Frazier was known for his heavy, short punches, especially his left hook, which was difficult to see and block. Unlike Liston, who was similarly powerful but lacked stamina, Frazier could fight fifteen rounds and still pack a powerful left hook at the very end.

Still, Ali didn't take Frazier seriously and didn't train particularly hard. He ran only two or three miles a day instead of the standard five or six. During sparring practice, he would lean against the ropes, protecting his face with his gloves and allowing his sparring partners to pummel him. Ali claimed he was toughening his body, but several boxing experts who watched him train thought it was just laziness.

66*Muhammad suffered when he wasn't allowed to fight, and I don't mean financially. Money was the least of it. He suffered because he loved boxing. . . . He's not bitter about the years he lost, and that amazes me.*99

—ANGELO DUNDEE, ALI'S TRAINER

Ali's psychological attacks were the only aspect of his fighting strategy that remained exactly the same. During Ali's period in exile, Frazier had supported him in his bid to regain his boxing license and, according to some sources, had even loaned him money. Once Frazier became an opponent, however, Ali turned against him. He dusted off the insults he had used against Liston and inserted Frazier's name: "Joe Frazier is too ugly to be champ. Joe Frazier is too dumb to be champ. The heavyweight champion should be smart and pretty, like me." A proud man, Frazier found it difficult to laugh off the taunts.

More hurtfully, Ali claimed that the black community didn't support Frazier: "Ninety-eight percent of my people are for me. They identify with my struggle . . . . If I win, they win. I lose, they lose. Anybody black who thinks Frazier can whup me is an Uncle Tom." Frazier, who had grown up dirt poor near Beaufort, South Carolina, in one of the oldest African American settlements in the nation, had done nothing to justify the "Uncle Tom" label. But to his dismay, it stuck. By 1971 Ali had become a powerful symbol of black pride and anti-Vietnam sentiment. Simply because he was fighting Ali, Frazier was unfairly painted as the opposite.

On the night of the "Fight of the Century," as it was billed, more than twenty thousand people packed Madison Square Garden, an indoor attendance record. The press area was crammed with six hundred reporters and photographers. Even former vice president Hubert Humphrey was there—and the only seat he could get was in the balcony. Around the world, three hundred million people in thirty-five foreign countries were tuned to the fight. In the dressing room, Ali revealed his prediction. Frazier would fall in six.

Frazier walked into the ring wearing a green-and-gold robe with the names of his five children on it. Ali wore white satin over red velvet trunks and white shoes with red tassels. Both men were cheered.

The first two rounds of the fight went well for Ali, who looked like he had never been away from the championship ring. But it was an illusion. By round three, he was back against the ropes. As Frazier threw vicious punches, Ali turned to the crowd and shook his head, signaling that the punches hadn't hurt. His fans laughed, but sportswriters didn't. Some said it was the worst round Ali had ever boxed in his pro career.

At times during the fight, glimpses of the old Ali appeared. In round nine, he caught a second wind and danced beautifully around Frazier. He won several rounds with ease, but he was inconsistent. He seemed drawn to the ropes as if by a magnetic force, absorbing punishment and conceding points.

Then, in round eleven, came the moment that most boxing experts had expected. Frazier hit Ali with his dreaded left hook. Ali's neck snapped and his legs wobbled. Frazier pushed him against the ropes and landed another left hook. Ali's legs buckled, and he nearly hit the canvas. At the bell, he was still on his feet, but he moved shakily back to his corner.

Ali rallied in the fourteenth, then in the fifteenth round, Frazier knocked him down with a left hook to his jaw. Ali was up by the count of three, his jaw visibly swollen. "That night, he was the most courageous fighter I'd ever seen," Ferdie Pacheco, recalled later. "He was going to get up if he was dead." Frazier was announced the winner by unanimous decision.

Ali's loss was bitter not only for him but also for millions of fans who saw the fight as much more than a boxing match. At the press conference the next day, Ali was philosophical. "Just lost a fight, that's all," he told reporters. "There are more important things to worry about in life." Privately he was crushed. "The whole time I wasn't allowed to fight, no matter what the authorities said, it felt like I was the heavyweight champion of the world," he recalled later. After he lost to Frazier, "I would have done anything except go against the will of Allah to get my title back again."

On June 28, 1971, the U.S. Supreme Court unanimously reversed Ali's conviction for refusing induction. All criminal charges pending against him were dismissed. Ali was free of the threat of imprisonment, and his passport was returned. He could focus all his energy on making his comeback.

In July 1971, Ali defeated Jimmy Ellis, who had won the elimination tournament for heavyweight champion when Ali was first stripped of his title. More wins followed, including rematches with Chuvalo and Patterson. But none of the fights was as easy for Ali as they would have been before his layoff.

DEER LAKE

In 1972 Ali opened Fighter's Heaven in Deer Lake, Pennsylvania. The remote camp included a gym, a house for Ali and his family, and cabins for sparring partners and guests. Like Moore's camp, it had boulders with the names of famous boxers on them, painted by Clay Sr. Ali trained at Deer Lake for the rest of his career.

Meanwhile, in early 1973, Frazier lost the heavyweight title to George Foreman. Foreman was a powerful puncher who knocked Frazier down six times in just two rounds. By then Ali had won ten fights in a row and seemed well on his way to challenging for the heavyweight title. Then came Ken Norton, a little-known African American fighter. Seriously underestimating his low-ranked opponent, Ali trained for just three weeks.

Ali and Norton, a former marine, fought on March 31, 1973, in San Diego, California, a deeply conservative naval town. The symbolism of the fight—draft dodger against ex-marine—was stark and obvious.

Ali was in trouble nearly from the beginning of the fight. In the second round, Norton threw a straight right that broke Ali's jaw—the first and only time he had broken a bone in the ring.

Refusing to quit, Ali ignored the pain and fought the whole twelve rounds.

At the end, the fight was nearly scored even. Norton dominated the final round to win by split decision. It was an upset of enormous proportions. Afterward Ali had to have ninety minutes of surgery on his jaw. The doctor could barely believe he had been able to fight in such a painful condition.

To Ali's fans, especially those who cared more about politics than boxing, the loss to Norton was more disheartening than the loss of the heavyweight title. Even his greatest fans lost faith that he would ever get his title back. Sportscaster Howard Cosell, a longtime supporter, was typical in his view: "Losing to Norton was the end of the road, as far as I could see," he said. Yet Ali surprised them all when six months later he fought Norton again and won a close but unanimous decision.

In January 1974, Ali fought Frazier for a second time in Madison Square Garden. This time there was no title at stake, only an increasingly bitter grudge match. Before the fight, Ali and Frazier appeared on Cosell's television show. When Ali called Frazier ignorant, they ended up in a near brawl, rolling off the stage and onto the studio floor.

During the fight itself, neither Frazier nor Ali managed to land any particularly damaging punches. Whenever Frazier tried to hit at short range, his specialty, Ali tied him up in a clinch. After twelve sluggish rounds, Ali was announced the winner by unanimous decision.

Just one man stood between Ali and his heavyweight title. He was George Foreman, once called "the baddest man on the planet" by *Sports Illustrated*. Foreman, seven years younger, had decided to become a boxer because he wanted to be like his hero, Muhammad Ali. Like Sonny Liston before him, Foreman was considered unbeatable. In forty professional fights, he had scored thirty-seven knockouts and no losses. His recent fights included victories over Frazier and Norton, both of whom had beaten Ali. "My opponents don't worry about losing," Foreman said at the time. "They worry about getting hurt."

The fight between Foreman and Ali was billed as the "Rumble in the Jungle." It was scheduled to take place in Kinshasa, Zaire (later renamed the Democratic Republic of the Congo), in central Africa. "I guess the top of Mount Everest was busy," one reporter complained in print. Ali nicknamed Foreman "the Mummy." In his prediction poem, he made an unusual political reference to former president Richard Nixon, who had recently left office after being caught lying. "You think the world was shocked when Nixon resigned?" Ali said. "Wait till I whip George Foreman's behind."

The people of Zaire adored Ali, who was always out in public, mingling with his fans. Foreman stayed in seclusion. On the morning of October 30, 1974—the fight was held at 4 A.M. so fans in the United States could watch it live—the stadium was filled with spectators chanting, "Ali, *bomaye*!" ("Ali, kill him!")

Ali's original plan mirrored his strategy against Liston. He would dance for six or seven rounds, then move in once Foreman was tired. But in the first round, Ali realized that was a young man's plan; he no longer had the stamina to dance that long. Instead, he settled on a risky new one. He'd retreat to the ropes and tire Foreman out by letting Foreman hit him. It was a strategy borrowed from his first trainer, Archie Moore, who had called it "tortoiseshell."

In the break after round one, Angelo Dundee—Ali's second and only other professional trainer—shouted at him to get off the ropes and start dancing. Ali replied coolly, "I know what I'm doing." In round two, he was on the ropes again, blocking some punches, leaning back to avoid others, and grimly absorbing the rest. Foreman's specialty, just like Liston's, was big punches— and Ali had proved with Liston that he could spot them coming. No matter how hard Foreman hit, Ali was able to prepare for each punch, ride it through, and look out for the next one.

But Ali didn't just take punches; he landed them as well. Fighting off the ropes, he won three of the first four rounds. "I was throwing the most punches," Foreman later recalled, "but I knew that in some way I was losing." At the beginning of the eighth round, Ali told Foreman, "Now it's my turn," and knocked him out. Ten years after he had beaten Sonny Liston, seven years after he had been stripped of his title, Ali was once again the heavyweight champion of the world. What won the fight, Ali told reporters, was his "rope-a-dope" strategy—and Foreman, unwittingly, had been the dope.

66*Muhammad amazed me, I'll admit it. He outthought me, he outfought me. That night, he was just the better man in the ring.*99

—GEORGE FOREMAN

Ali's triumph over Foreman marked the final stage of his public transformation from enemy to hero. "Almost overnight," one sportswriter wrote, "he became the most popular man on the planet."

In 1967 *Ring* magazine had chosen not to designate a "Fighter of the Year" in order to deny the honor to Ali. "Cassius Clay most emphatically is not to be held up as an example to the youngsters of the United States," it had stated. In 1974 Ali was not only named *Ring*'s Fighter of the Year but also *Sports Illustrated*'s Sportsman of the Year. He was awarded the Hickok Belt, given to the nation's outstanding pro athlete.

The media joined in the frenzy, describing Ali as a folk hero. "It is time to recognize Ali for what he is," one reporter gushed in the *New York Post*, "the greatest athlete of his time and maybe all time and one of the most important and brave men of all American time."

Then came an honor that would have been inconceivable just a few years before. On December 10, 1974, President Gerald Ford invited Ali to the White House. Ford was a boxing fan who genuinely wanted to meet Ali. More important, he wanted to help heal the wounds of the 1960s, when Ali had been such a powerful symbol of a divided nation.

Ali too was ready to put his years of exile and struggle behind him: "Now that I got my championship back," he told his best friend, photographer Howard Bingham, "every day is something special. I wake up in the morning, and no matter what the weather is like, every day is a sunny day."

Chapter Nine

Triumphs and Humiliations

Ali was once again heavyweight champion, but his feud with Joe Frazier continued to burn. Ali never forgave Frazier for taking the crown he thought was rightfully his. He continued to call Frazier ugly, ignorant, and, worst of all, an Uncle Tom. Frazier, who was as proud of his race as Ali, deeply resented the insults. "It's real hatred," Frazier told reporters. "I want to hurt him. I don't want to knock him out. I want to take his heart out."

Ali nicknamed their third and final fight, staged in the Philippines, the "Thrilla in Manila." (Manila is the capital city of the Philippines.) At the press conference announcing the bout, Ali mocked Frazier's southern accent. Nicknaming Frazier "the Gorilla," Ali told reporters, "It will be a killer and a chiller and a thrilla when I get the Gorilla in Manila." Then he pulled a small rubber gorilla out of his pocket and pretended to beat it up:

"Come on, Gorilla; we're in Manila. Come on, Gorilla; this is a thrilla." Most of the reporters laughed, despite the fact that the gorilla image revived an ugly racial stereotype of blacks.

❝ While [Ali's] latest struggle has been to convince blacks that 'black is beautiful,' he always knew where to hit black opponents before fights. Some new variant of 'black is ugly' is where he would hit them. ❞

—JOSÉ TORRES

The match itself was almost overshadowed by Ali's personal life. During his marriage to Belinda, Ali had numerous affairs. Having affairs went against NOI teachings. Ali had even fathered two daughters, Miya and Khaliah, with two different women. While Belinda remained in Chicago, Ali had traveled to Manila with his girlfriend, Veronica Porche, an aspiring actress.

At the time, Ali was protected by an old-fashioned code of ethics in journalism. Reporters didn't write about the private lives of public men. But in the Philippines, Ali didn't even try to keep his private life private. When he and Frazier were invited to meet Filipino President Ferdinand Marcos, Ali brought along his parents, his trainer, and Veronica. Marcos complimented Ali on the beauty of his wife, and everyone was too embarrassed to explain who Veronica actually was.

When one reporter finally wrote about Veronica, Ali held a press conference to defend himself. Twenty-four hours later, Belinda was on a plane to Manila. After a noisy argument, Belinda flew back to Chicago on the same plane she had arrived on. She eventually filed for divorce.

Ali-Frazier III took place on October 1, 1975 in Quezon City, six miles outside Manila. The fight was held at 10:45 A.M. so that it could be shown live in the United States at a convenient time. The air-conditioning was broken in the 25,000-seat Philippines Coliseum, which was jammed and sweltering.

The fight was long, dramatic, and extremely brutal. The fighting was so tough from the opening bell that many boxing experts expected it to end quickly. But with so much personal dislike between Ali and Frazier, neither one was prepared to give up.

Ali dominated the early rounds. He outboxed Frazier, landing sharp clean blows that staggered him several times. Then the fight shifted, and Frazier began to dominate. In round six, he hit Ali in the head with a left hook that one reporter described as "the hardest punch I've ever seen." When Ali recovered, he looked up at Frazier and said, "They told me Joe Frazier was washed up." Frazier replied calmly, "They lied." For the next five rounds, Frazier released all of his pent-up rage against Ali.

In the eleventh round, Ali staged a near-miraculous rally. For the final four rounds, he fought with precision and fury. In the twelfth round, Ali landed six consecutive punches to Frazier's head, then moments later landed eight more. In the thirteenth, he knocked Frazier's protective mouthpiece into the crowd.

By the fourteenth round, both of Frazier's eyes were beginning to close. Ali's punches were landing cleanly, Frazier couldn't see them, and he was spitting blood. At the end of the round, Frazier's trainer made the decision to stop the fight, even though Frazier wanted to battle on. Ali said later, "Frazier quit just before I did. I didn't think I could fight anymore."

For boxing experts, the "Thrilla in Manila" marked the last of Ali's three great fights, along with the heavyweight championship win over Liston and the "Rumble in the Jungle" against Foreman. Ali-Frazier III was memorable for its shifting momentum, its savagery, and its final moment, when both great fighters sat battered on their stools. Many journalists described it as the most exciting prizefight in modern history. Ferdie Pacheco, Ali's doctor, called it the toughest fight he had ever seen. "Man, I hit him with punches that'd bring down the walls of a city," Frazier said afterward.

After the Frazier fight, Ali fought various matches with little-known opponents, including Great Britain's Richard Dunn. Ali knocked Dunn down five times before ending the fight in the fifth round. They were the last knockdowns of Ali's professional career.

On September 28, 1976, Ali fought Ken Norton for a third
time in New York's Yankee Stadium. Norton did well in the early
rounds and was ahead until round eight. Then Ali took over,
winning every round but the twelfth. He came on especially
strong in the last round to win the extremely close fight. Despite
the win, even Ali's most devoted fans had to admit he was obvi-
ously in decline. Ali's timing was off, his punches lacked power,
and he tired easily. *Sports Illustrated* declared, "There is no ques-
tion now that Ali is through as a fighter."

On June 19, 1977, Ali and Veronica Porche were married in
Los Angeles. By then the couple had a ten-month-old daughter,
Hana. They later had another daughter, Laila.

On September 29, Ali defended his title against Earnie
Shavers in Madison Square Garden. Since Foreman's retirement,

Shavers was regarded as the hardest puncher in boxing. The fight, broadcast on NBC, was massively popular—three out of four American televisions in use were tuned to the fight.

In the second round, Shavers hit Ali with a powerful right. "Next to Joe Frazier," Ali said later, "that was the hardest I ever got hit." He managed to fight for the entire fifteen rounds, though he was so exhausted at the beginning of round fifteen that he could barely stand. The judges scored the close fight for Ali.

❝ *Of all the men I fought in boxing, Sonny Liston was the scariest; George Foreman was the most powerful; Floyd Patterson was the most skilled as a boxer. But the roughest and toughest was Joe Frazier.* **❞**

—Muhammad Ali

At thirty-five, Ali's skills had deteriorated to such a point that only his courage kept him on his feet. Once he had been proud of the fact that he was so quick, his opponents couldn't land a punch. Now Ali prided himself on how much pummeling he could take. True, Ali won fights. But the repeated blows to the head and the body were beginning to have an effect.

The day after the Shavers bout, Teddy Brenner, who planned the fights at Madison Square Garden, privately urged Ali to retire.

When Ali was noncommittal, Brenner told reporters at the post-fight press conference that he would never schedule another fight for Ali at Madison Square Garden. "The trick in boxing is to get out at the right time, and the fifteenth round last night was the right time for Ali," he said. Soon afterward Ferdie Pacheco, Ali's doctor, resigned over concerns about Ali's health—his kidneys were no longer functioning properly—after Ali refused to take him seriously.

By this time, Ali was being scheduled only for "easy fights," but even the easy fights were hard on his damaged body and increasingly hard for him to win. His next "easy fight" was supposed to be Leon Spinks, a gold medalist from the 1976 Montreal Olympics in Canada. Like Foreman, Spinks had idolized Ali as a young man.

Ali at first turned down the chance to fight Spinks, who had fought just seven professional matches and wasn't even ranked in the top ten. Later Ali changed his mind, wanting to add Spinks to the list of gold medalists he had defeated: Floyd Patterson, Joe Frazier, and George Foreman. Despite Ali's attempt to interest the press in the gold-medal story, the fight was considered too lopsided to generate much coverage.

During the fight, Ali gave away the early rounds, hoping his rope-a-dope strategy would wear Spinks out. But Spinks was young and strong. Realizing that he was losing, Ali fought back desperately in the last round and even managed to back Spinks up against the ropes. But it was much too late. Spinks was chosen as the winner by a split decision. Ali had finally lost his title in the ring.

"I messed up; I was lousy," Ali said at the press conference afterward. "But I don't want to take anything away from Spinks. He fought a good fight and never quit. He made fools out of everybody, even me." Ali demanded, and got, an immediate rematch.

After the contract was signed, Ali embarked on a twelve-day goodwill tour of the Soviet Union and south central Asia. In Moscow, when he boxed an exhibition match against amateur Soviet boxers, he was clearly having trouble. Still, he refused to admit it might be time to retire. Back in the United States, Ali told reporters that Spinks had merely borrowed his title.

In preparation for the rematch against Spinks, Ali trained hard. He ran three to five miles every morning, did 200 sit-ups a day, and sparred hundreds of rounds. "All my life, I knew the day would come when I'd have to kill myself," Ali said at the time. "I always dreaded it, and now it's here. I've never suffered like I'm forcing myself to suffer now." Meanwhile the party-loving Spinks was enjoying being champion—anywhere except in the gym. He trained just ten days for the rematch.

On September 15, 1978, the Superdome in New Orleans, Louisiana, was packed with more than sixty thousand fans. It was the largest indoor fight attendance in history. Ali's plan was to jab and throw as many punches as possible at the end of each round to impress the judges and give Spinks something to think about during rounds.

It was a slow, sluggish fight, but Ali was in control, especially at the end. Ali won the fight by unanimous decision. Spinks was one of the first to raise Ali's right arm in victory.

Afterward several sportswriters pointed out that Ali hadn't really won the championship—Spinks had lost it. Nonetheless, Muhammad Ali had set a new record. He was the first man to win the heavyweight championship of the world three times.

Chapter | Ten

Technical Knockout

On June 26, 1979, nine months after defeating Spinks, thirty-seven-year-old Ali announced that he was retired. "Everybody gets old," he told reporters. "This time, I'm thinking about my family, my children, the record books. I'd be a fool to fight again."

For two years after the Spinks bout, Ali didn't box. He turned to his other talents, speaking and acting. Ali also traveled the world, raising money for charity and meeting with heads of state. At a time when the United States and the Soviet Union were still mired in the Cold War, Ali met Soviet leader Leonid Brezhnev.

In early 1980, Ali began talking about a boxing comeback. The decision was controversial. By his second year of retirement, Ali weighed 255 pounds and was completely out of shape. His mother said publicly that she did not want her son to return to boxing, as did Ferdie Pacheco. "Even Muhammad Ali is human and subject to the laws of nature," Pacheco declared.

Against most advice, Ali signed to fight world champion Larry Holmes. Holmes, a friend and admirer, had worked at Ali's training camp as a sparring partner from 1973 to 1975. Holmes didn't want to fight Ali. He agreed with those who thought Ali should remain in retirement. But he felt he had no choice since the public wouldn't respect him if he turned down Ali's challenge.

During the usual prefight buildup, Ali nicknamed Holmes "the Peanut" because of the shape of his head. "I'm going to shell him and send him to Plains, Georgia," he told reporters. Ali also claimed that he sparred with one hand behind his back and that he hadn't decided if he was going to fight Holmes with one hand or two. But now even Ali's psychological punches were no longer effective. Holmes knew Ali so well, he could finish Ali's lines before he did.

Despite Ali's joking, there was more and more public concern about the state of his health. Before the Nevada State Athletic Commission would license the bout, Ali was required to undergo a two-day evaluation at the prestigious Mayo Clinic in Rochester, Minnesota.

Ali told the Mayo Clinic doctors that his speech had been slurred for the past decade and that he sometimes staggered when he walked. During medical testing, Ali didn't hop particularly well and had some problems touching his finger to his nose. Despite these obvious danger signs—worrisome for anyone, let alone a heavyweight boxer challenging for the championship—he was given a license to fight.

On October 2, 1980, Ali and Holmes fought in a temporary arena in the parking lot of Caesar's Palace, a Las Vegas casino and hotel. The nearly 25,000 fans who had gathered to watch the bout were soon disappointed. From round one, Ali could barely defend himself. "After the first round, I knew I was in trouble," Ali recalled later. "I was tired, nothing left at all."

❝No matter where I go, everybody recognizes my face and knows my name. People love and admire me; they look up to me. That's a lot of power and influence for one man to have, so I know I have a responsibility to use my fame the right way.❞

—MUHAMMAD ALI

The fight was so lopsided, several times Holmes looked over at the referee as if asking him to stop it. Holmes was deliberately holding back, trying not to injure Ali. The judges awarded Holmes every round until the fight was stopped at the end of the tenth. "I embarrassed myself," Ali said afterward. "I felt embarrassed for all my fans. I fought like an old man who was washed up."

After the match, the victorious Holmes was depressed. He went to Ali's hotel room, where Holmes told Ali that he was still the greatest and he loved him.

Four days after the fight, Ali checked into the UCLA Medical Center, where he told the doctors he was taking medication for a thyroid condition. Thinking the pills were like vitamins, Ali had taken three times the prescribed amount. The UCLA doctors found no evidence of a thyroid problem; with so much inappropriate medication in his system, Ali was lucky even to have survived the Holmes fight.

Incredibly Ali still didn't want to retire. Some of his advisers were telling him that he had fought so badly because of the thyroid drug, not because of his age. "I thought I should go out of boxing with a win," Ali said later. "And if I couldn't go out with a win, at least I wanted to be throwing punches at the end."

Ali was scheduled to fight Trevor Berbick on December 11, 1981. Once again promoters couldn't find a U.S. city to host it. The problem this time was Ali's obvious health problems. In the end, the fight was scheduled for the Bahamas, an island country off the coast of Florida.

For a second time, Ali's mother publicly pleaded with him not to fight, and the rest of the nation seemed to agree with her. The three major U.S. television networks refused to show the bout. There was no interest in closed-circuit broadcasts for movie theaters. Several sportswriters who had covered Ali for decades announced they would boycott it.

Berbick was an unimpressive fighter, but he easily outboxed Ali. When Berbick won the fight by unanimous decision, Ali admitted that time had finally caught up with him. Now, unlike after the Holmes fight, he could make no excuses. "I'm happy I'm still pretty," he said. "I came out all right for an old man."

Soon afterward Ali returned to Louisville for a visit. There he met an old friend, Yolanda "Lonnie" Williams, for lunch. Lonnie's family lived across the street from Ali's family, and their mothers were best friends. Lonnie had heard about Ali's condition, but she was shocked when she saw him in person. During their brief visit, Ali stumbled several times. Lonnie moved to Los Angeles soon afterward and spent much of her time caring for Ali.

In his retirement, Ali's Islamic faith deepened. He became a self-described "true believer" around 1983. "Before that, I thought I was a true believer, but I wasn't," he said later. "I fit my religion to do what I wanted."

In September 1984, Ali checked into a New York City hospital for a thorough evaluation. He complained of slurred speech, trembling in his hands, and exhaustion that didn't go away no matter how much he slept. Eventually Ali was diagnosed with Parkinson's disease, a neurological disorder. Its main symptoms include a tremor, slow movement, impaired balance, and rigid muscles, including facial muscles—known as "masked face"—and the muscles used in speech.

Some doctors who examined Ali have blamed his condition on all the head shots he took as a boxer. Other experts have argued that Ali had an inherited predisposition to the disease. In his autobiography, *The Soul of a Butterfly*, Ali denies that boxing was to blame: "I would have had Parkinson's if I had been a baker. There aren't many boxers that have Parkinson's, and there are lots of people who have Parkinson's who've never even seen a boxing match, let alone been in one."

ALI'S CHILDREN

Ali's youngest daughter, Laila, became a professional boxer in 1999. By 2005 she had fought twenty-one bouts, scoring eighteen knockouts and no losses.

Several of his other children have become authors. Ali's 2002 autobiography, *The Soul of a Butterfly*, was cowritten with Hana. In 2003 Maryum wrote a children's biography of her father, *I Shook Up the World*. In 2005 Rasheda wrote *I'll Hold Your Hand So You Won't Fall: A Child's Guide to Parkinson's Disease*, for which Ali provided the foreword.

The terrible irony of Ali's condition is that it robbed him of his most noted gifts. Once he recited poetry and shouted predictions like a street preacher; now he had difficulty speaking with family and friends. Once he moved with incredible grace and speed; now he stumbled. His left hand, which threw out thousands of powerful left jabs, shook almost continuously. And Ali's "pretty" face, which he pulled into a thousand expressions while hamming it up for the cameras, had frozen into a mask.

Surprisingly, Ali wasn't bitter about his condition, accepting it as he had accepted all the other strange fortunes and misfortunes of his life. "I know why this happened," Ali told one sportswriter. "God is showing me, and showing you, that I'm just a man, just like everybody else."

Epilogue

The People's Champion

After years of struggling to make their marriage work, Ali and Veronica divorced in July 1986. Ali and Lonnie were married on November 19, 1986, in Louisville and later adopted a son, Asaad. An intelligent, educated woman, Lonnie gave up her own career to care for Ali and manage his business affairs.

Despite his retirement and the difficulties of his physical condition, Ali refused to slow down. He continued to travel the world, making public appearances and raising money for charity—according to one estimate, more than $50 million since he retired from the ring.

Ali continued to serve as an unofficial ambassador for the United States. In November 1990, as the prospect of war between the United States and Iraq loomed, Ali met with Iraqi leader Saddam Hussein. Ali hoped that as a fellow Muslim, he might be able to promote dialogue and forestall armed conflict.

While unable to prevent the Gulf War, Ali returned to the United States with fifteen of the estimated three hundred hostages then being held by Iraq.

In 1996 Ali made an emotional appearance at the Olympic Games in Atlanta, Georgia—the first city where he had been allowed to fight after his exile. Just a handful of people knew before the opening ceremony that Ali would light the Olympic flame. When he stepped out of the shadows on the platform, the crowd of eighty-three thousand went wild with applause. Some spectators, including President Bill Clinton, even cried. "As his left arm shook," one reporter wrote in *Sports Illustrated*, "he lit the flame and choked the breath of a nation." After the ceremony, Ali was unable to sleep; he sat in his hotel room holding the Olympic torch until dawn. Later in the Atlanta Games, Ali was presented with a replacement gold medal.

The following year, Ali made an appearance at the Academy Awards. The 1996 film *When We Were Kings*, about the "Rumble in the Jungle," won an Oscar for best documentary.

In 1998 Ali was named a United Nations Messenger of Peace. Ali's efforts for peace also included issuing a statement the day after the September 11, 2001, terrorist attacks on New York City and Washington, D.C. "As an American Muslim, I want to express my deep sadness and anguish at the tremendous loss of life that occurred on Tuesday," the statement read in part.

"Islam is a religion of peace. Islam does not promote terrorism or the killing of people."

In November 2005, the Muhammad Ali Center, a ninety-three-thousand-square-foot facility dedicated to Ali's life, opened in Louisville. Intended to be not a museum but a "place of ideas," the center includes six exhibits on values Ali feels strongly about: respect, conviction, confidence, dedication, spirituality, and giving. In an area designed to look like Ali's training camp, visitors can learn to hit a speed bag and see Ali's replacement gold medal. Other exhibits let visitors see a replay of any of Ali's fights or be projected into Ali's 1996 Olympic torch-lighting experience.

In the first half of his boxing career, Ali was the genius in the ring who did everything wrong, according to the experts—then he confounded them all by winning. In the second half, after his youth had been stolen for political reasons, Ali reinvented his fighting style and won no longer by quickness but by stamina, strategy, and bravery.

"When will they ever have another fighter who writes poems, predicts rounds, beats everybody, makes people laugh, makes people cry, and is as tall and extra pretty as me?" Ali, always his own biggest fan, once asked. "In the history of the world from the beginning of time, there's never been another fighter like me."

PERSONAL STATISTICS

Name:

Cassius Marcellus Clay (1942–1964), Muhammad Ali (1964–)

Nicknames:

Louisville Lip, G. G.

Born:

January 17, 1942

Height:

6'3"

Weight:

210–231 lbs.

Residence:

Berrien Springs, Michigan

SELECTED FIGHT RECORD

Year	Date	Opponent	Location	Result	World
1960	Oct 29	Tunney Hunsaker	Louisville, Kentucky	WD6	
	Dec 27	Herb Siler	Miami Beach, Florida	KO4	
1961	Jan 17	Anthony Sperti	Miami Beach, Florida	TKO3	
	June 26	Duke Sabedong	Las Vegas, Nevada	W10	
	July 22	Alonzo Johnson	Louisville, Kentucky	WD10	
	Nov 29	Willie Besmanoff	Louisville, Kentucky	TKO7	
1962	Feb 10	Sonny Banks	New York, New York	TKO4	
	Feb 28	Don Warner	Miami Beach, Florida	TKO4	
	Nov 15	Archie Moore	Los Angeles, California	TKO4	
1963	Jan 24	Charlie Powell	Pittsburgh, Pennsylvania	KO3	
	Mar 13	Doug Jones	New York, New York	WD10	
	June 18	Henry Cooper	London, England	TKO5	
1964	Feb 25	Sonny Liston	Miami Beach, Florida	TKO7	WORLD
1965	May 25	Sonny Liston	Lewiston, Maine	KO1	WORLD
	Nov 22	Floyd Patterson	Las Vegas, Nevada	TKO12	WORLD
1966	Mar 29	George Chuvalo	Toronto, Canada	WD15	WORLD
	May 21	Henry Cooper	London, England	TKO6	WORLD
	Aug 6	Brian London	London, England	KO3	WORLD
	Sept 10	Karl Mildenberger	Frankfurt, Germany	TKO12	WORLD
	Nov 14	Cleveland Williams	Houston, Texas	TKO3	WORLD
1967	Feb 6	Ernie Terrell	Houston, Texas	W15	WORLD
	Mar 22	Zora Folley	New York, New York	KO7	WORLD
1970	Oct 26	Jerry Quarry	Atlanta, Georgia	TKO3	
	Dec 7	Oscar Bonavena	New York, New York	TKO15	
1971	Mar 8	Joe Frazier	New York, New York	LD15	WORLD
	July 26	Jimmy Ellis	Houston, Texas	TKO12	

Key: **WD**: Win by decision; **LD**: Loss by decision; **KO**: Knockout; **TKO**: Technical knockout; **WORLD**: World championship bout

1971	Nov 17	Buster Mathis	Houston, Texas	WD12	
	Dec 26	Jurgen Blin	Zurich, Switzerland	KO7	
1972	Apr 1	Mac Foster	Tokyo, Japan	WD15	
	May 1	George Chuvalo	Vancouver, Canada	WD12	
	June 27	Jerry Quarry	Las Vegas, Nevada	TKO7	
	July 19	Alvin Lewis	Dublin, Ireland	TKO11	
	Sept 20	Floyd Patterson	New York, New York	TKO7	
	Nov 21	Bob Foster	Stateline, Nevada	TKO8	
1973	Feb 14	Joe Bugner	Las Vegas, Nevada	WD12	
	Mar 31	Ken Norton	San Diego, California	LD12	
	Sept 10	Ken Norton	Los Angeles, California	WD12	
	Oct 20	Rudy Lubbers	Jakarta, Indonesia	WD12	
1974	Jan 28	Joe Frazier	New York, New York	WD12	
	Oct 30	George Foreman	Kinshasa, Zaire	KO8	WORLD
1975	Mar 24	Chuck Wepner	Cleveland, Ohio	TKO15	WORLD
	May 16	Ron Lyle	Las Vegas, Nevada	TKO11	WORLD
	June 30	Joe Bugner	Kuala Lumpur, Malaysia	WD15	WORLD
	Oct 1	Joe Frazier	Manila, Philippines	TKO14	WORLD
1976	Feb 20	Jean-Pierre Coopman	San Juan, Puerto Rico	KO5	WORLD
	Apr 30	Jimmy Young	Landover, Maryland	WD15	WORLD
	May 24	Richard Dunn	Munich, Germany	TKO5	WORLD
	Sept 28	Ken Norton	New York, New York	WD15	WORLD
1977	May 16	Alfredo Evangelista	Landover, Maryland	WD15	WORLD
	Sept 29	Earnie Shavers	New York, New York	WD15	WORLD
1978	Feb 15	Leon Spinks	Las Vegas, Nevada	LD15	WORLD
	Sept 15	Leon Spinks	New Orleans, Louisiana	WD15	WORLD
1980	Oct 2	Larry Holmes	Las Vegas, Nevada	TKO'd11	WORLD
1981	Dec 11	Trevor Berbick	Nassau, Bahamas	LD10	

Key: **WD:** Win by decision; **LD:** Loss by decision; **KO:** Knockout; **TKO:** Technical knockout; **WORLD:** World championship bout

BIBLIOGRAPHY

Ali: The Whole Story. Turner Network Television, 1996.

Ali, Muhammad, with Hana Yasmeen Ali. *The Soul of a Butterfly: Reflections on Life's Journey.* New York: Simon & Schuster, 2004.

Dennis, Felix, and Don Atyeo. *Muhammad Ali: The Glory Years.* New York: Miramax Books, 2003.

Early, Gerald. *The Muhammad Ali Reader.* Hopewell, NJ: Ecco Press, 1998.

Hauser, Thomas. *Muhammad Ali: His Life and Times.* New York: Simon & Schuster, 1991.

Marqusee, Mike. *Redemption Song: Muhammad Ali and the Spirit of the Sixties.* London: Verso, 1999.

Miller, Davis. *The Tao of Muhammad Ali.* New York: Warner Books, 1996.

Reemtsma, Jan Philipp. *More Than a Champion: The Style of Muhammad Ali.* New York: Vintage Books, 1998.

Remnick, David. *King of the World.* New York: Random House, 1998.

WEB SITES

Muhammad Ali—The Greatest of All Time

www.ali.com

Muhammad Ali's official web site features fight statistics, news about Ali, letters written to him, and answers to frequently asked questions.

Muhammad Ali Center

www.alicenter.org

This is the official site of the Ali Center, which opened in Louisville in November 2005. It includes information about visiting.

Courier-Journal.com

www.courier-journal.com/ali/index.html

This Louisville newspaper maintains an archive of articles about Ali, a hometown hero.

CNN/SI—Century's Best—Muhammad Ali SI Cover Gallery

sportsillustrated.cnn.com/centurys_best/boxing/gallery/ali/main/index.html

Sports Illustrated *presents thirty-five covers featuring Ali from 1963 to 1998.*

INDEX